DATING FOR MEN MADE EASY

15 KEYS TO CRUSH YOUR DATING LIFE AND MAKE YOU MORE SUCCESSFUL

EASOP SR.

Copyright © 2024 Essence Love Publishing, LLC

All rights reserved. No part of this book may be reproduced in any form without permission from the publisher or author, except as permitted by U.S. copyright law.

ISBN 979-8-218-56180-2
Library of Congress Control Number: 2024924676
Printed in: United States of America
First printing edition 2024

Design and layout: Wael Morgan
Author: Easop Sr.
Contributing Editor: FAYMUS

Published by: Essence Love Publishing, LLC
3093 Broadway PH 42
Oakland, Ca. 94611

Website: www.datingformenmadeeasy.com
email: datingformenmadeeasy@gmail.com

Dedication

*In loving memory of my
Mother, my angel, and my
brothers Rodney and Byron...
Gone but not forgotten...*

*To My Dad, and three kids,
Easop Jr, Essence, and Easi...*

TABLE OF CONTENTS

Introduction 5

Key 1: Setting The Table (PREPARATION) 10

Key 2: Keep It Real (Honesty) 16

Key 3: Walk Like A Star (Confidence) 21

Key 4: Look Good, Feel Good (Appearance) 27

Key 5: Treat Her Like A Lady (Chivalry) 33

Key 6: Aretha Franklin (Respect) 39

Key 7: Why So Serious (Humor) 44

Key 8: I'm All Ears (A Good Listener) 50

Key 9: Take Control (Planning) 55

Key 10: Weird Science (Know Your Type) 60

Key 11: The R Word (Rejection) 65

Key 12: Go Fish (The Catch) 71

Key 13: Talk A Good Game (Communication) 77

Key 14: Don't Chase, Replace (Walk Away) 82

Key 15: Don't Be Weird (Red Flags) 87

Knock It Out The Park (Sex) *Bonus Key 92

Conclusion 98

INTRODUCTION

This is a dating book. I emphasize. This is a dating book, not a *relationship* book. Let's not get it twisted. We're not here to talk about how to make it to your fifth anniversary or how to keep the love alive. This book is about *the chase*. It's about the game before the love story, where you're out there, getting to know women, seeing where it leads. Whether it's casual, serious, or just seeing what's up, this book is meant to help you navigate the crazy world of dating as a man.

Let's talk about *what dating actually is*. Sure, you probably have your own idea of what dating looks like, but at its core, dating is the social act of getting to know someone first as a friend, and then romantically. During the dating phase, you're assessing compatibility, figuring out if there's chemistry, and seeing if you're interested in taking things further. It's a process of learning about each other's personalities, goals, and lifestyles. Are you both on the same wavelength or are you just wasting each other's time?

Now, dating can look a thousand different ways. You might go out for drinks, catch a movie, hit the gym together, take a casual stroll in the park, or whatever you're into. Sometimes, it's casual; sometimes, it's more intentional. But at the end of the day, you're trying to build a connection. *It's about that bond.* I like to think of it as collecting data because that's what dating essentially is. Whether you're in a big city or a small town, the dating game is the same.

Here's the thing, dating today is complicated. It's full of twists and turns, and if you don't know what you're doing, it can feel like you're walking through a minefield. Back in the day, you mainly met women at church, bars, nightclubs, work, gyms, through friends, or at your local grocery store. Today? It's a whole different ballgame. With dating apps and social media, you have more access to women than ever before. Want to slide into a girl's DMs? Go for it. Feeling lucky on Tinder? Swipe away. But to all of this, as with anything these days, there's a catch. Because social media has turned dating into a *sport*. It's big business now. People spend hours crafting the perfect online persona just to catch someone's eye. Hell, people even pay for premium features just to get noticed on some dating websites.

The sad truth about today's dating world is you never really know the real woman behind the dating profile until you meet her face to face, and that's usually where most guys fumble the bag. You were all confident and charismatic via text, but the moment she's sitting across the table from you, you're sweating bullets and rambling about the six best ways to grill a steak. We've got to fix that.

So, let's cut to the chase. When it comes to dating, most men are either looking to get laid or find "the one." There's no shame in either goal, but you've got to be honest about where you're at. Whatever the case, this book is for you. No BS, no fluff. Just practical advice to give you the edge when it comes to dating.

All this easy access to women online is both a blessing and a curse. I mean, you can shoot your shot at anyone these days by simply sliding in their DMs. But again, people can be anything they want to be online, which means you have to be smart about how you move. There's a reason we have terms like "catfishing" now. Someone might look like a model online, but in person, not so much. And that's why being intentional and authentic in your dating game is more important than ever.

So, you're out there dating or attempting to date. Maybe you're fresh out of a breakup or just looking to refresh your skills. Either way, this book is your wingman. I'm talking to the guy who's just dipping his toes back into the dating pool after a divorce or breakup, to the guy who's never really dated and feels a little lost, and to the guy who's just trying to sharpen his game.

I've been around the block a few times myself. Seventeen years in the dating world, in and out of relationships, and let me tell you, I've seen it all. Before that, I was married at 20 for twelve years, so yeah, I know a thing or two about women. Whether it's traditional dating, online dating, or even some more unconventional situations (I'll save the polygamy stories for another time), trust me, I've experienced just about everything. I've got stories for days, some good, some bad, some straight-up wild. I've seen how dating has evolved, how apps and social media have changed the game, and how men and women interact differently now. And I'm here to help you make sense of it all.

But why should you listen to me?

Well, I've lived every piece of advice I give in this book. I've truly lived it. I'm not some self-proclaimed expert who went to school to study relationships. Nope, I'm just a regular guy with a lot of dating experience. In fact, I've been called a "ladies' man" by plenty of people, and I've earned that title by figuring out what works with women and being around them. I've been on dates where I've sat across from two or three women at the same time (yeah, that's right), and I've had my fair share of one-night stands with women I met just hours before. So, I know what I'm talking about.

I've also worked with and managed models over the years, so I've seen firsthand what women want and need. I've been privy to countless stories about men and their dating blunders. And trust me, a lot of you are making mistakes you don't even know you're making. That's where I come in— I'm here to give you the playbook on how to avoid those pitfalls and start crushing it in the dating scene.

In essence, what I'm teaching you in this book is that the dating game has rules. Don't expect fancy psychology, degree terminology, or case studies backed by years of academic research. We're not diving into the science of attraction here (well, maybe just a little). We're talking straight-up, no-nonsense advice that works. The thing is, women want a guy who knows what he's doing. You see, dating is about learning the psychology of women and speaking their language. If you want to win the game, you've got to understand the rules.

I want you to crush the dating game. Just as every hitter steps up to the plate with a plan, I will equip you to go into the dating game with a strategy. You can't just walk into a date without knowing how you're going to handle things. Are you there to just hook up, or are you trying to lock down something serious? What's your intention? Because your intention will determine your approach. Either way, you have to understand that dating isn't just about you. It's about understanding her, too. What makes her tick? What are her likes, her dislikes, her ambitions?

There are a lot of beautiful women in the world looking for a man who possesses the right qualities, skillset, confidence, swag, and mouthpiece to win her, but you have to be polished, intentional, and come with the right approach. Remember, don't step to the plate if you're not ready to swing the bat! You have to speak their language and learn the psychology of a woman. Dating takes a certain social skill, and level of understanding. There's a moxy to it.

If you're the type of guy who's socially awkward, or if you struggle to get that second or third date, this book is for you. If you're not getting laid as much as you want, or if you're looking to lock down that perfect 10 you've been chasing, then this book will help you level up your game. Dating is about confidence, and confidence comes from knowledge. The more you know about the opposite sex, the better your odds of success. Some of these principles are universal, but I expand on them in an easy-to-follow way.

The 15 easy keys in this book are universal principles but laid out in an easy-to-follow way without all the fancy, over-the-top jargon. In addition to these 15 keys that headline each chapter, are hidden gems in every chapter, that go into even greater detail. So actually, there are more than 15 keys that are laid out in this book!! I even took the time to provide you with a bonus chapter on sex. There's no secret formula. Just apply these simple keys and additional gems to your dating life and you'll find yourself getting more dates, more connections, and more chances to get to know the women you're interested in.

At the end of the day, dating is a skill. You need to be polished, have your swag on point, and know how to approach women in a way that works. You can't just walk up to the plate and hope for the best. You've got to have the right game plan and I've got you covered.

KEY 1: SETTING THE TABLE (PREPARATION)

Alright, fellas, let's get into it. Before we jump into the deep end of the dating pool, we've got to do some prep work. Think of it as *setting the table* before the meal. You can't just have a fork on the table. You need a knife, a spoon, a plate, a glass, etc. A stable man is a man who has his table set.

What does this mean?

If you're going to jump into the dating pool and make the most of it, you need to make sure you're ready mentally, emotionally, and financially. You can't be stumbling into this thing half-prepared. If you're not stable in these three key areas, you shouldn't even be out here dating. This might sound harsh, but I have to be real with you.

Now, I'm not here to judge where you are in life. Every man's journey is different. But here's the deal: I want you to have the best possible experience when it comes to dating, and being stable in these three areas is going to help you do just that. Think of it like building a house. You wouldn't build a house on a shaky foundation, right? The same logic applies to dating. If you're not on solid ground, you're setting yourself up for disaster. When you've got your ish together in these three areas, you're not just bringing stability into your own life, you're also offering stability to the women you're dating.

Stability equals options. What man doesn't want more options when it comes to the pool of women he gets to choose from? When you're grounded in all three, not only are you going to have better experiences, but you'll also have more options. But, you've got to make sure you set your table right. So, let's talk about these three key things.

1. The Mental Game: Check Yourself Before You Wreck Yourself

Let's start with the mental side of things because if your head's not in the right place, everything else is going to fall apart. Mental health is finally getting the attention it deserves, especially for men. I know many of us were raised to "tough it out," keep our emotions bottled up, and act like nothing ever phases us. I get it. I was raised that way, and I bet a lot of you were too. But let's be real, that mindset is a one-way ticket to disaster. Bottling up your emotions and walking around carrying the weight of the world on your shoulders doesn't make you tough. On the contrary, it makes you a ticking timebomb and you will explode when you least expect it.

This isn't a mental health book, but I'd be doing you a disservice if I didn't talk about how important your mental state is when it comes to dating. If you're not in a good headspace, you can't present the best version of yourself. A major part of dating is making a good first impression. You want to come across as confident, calm, and in control. If you've got unresolved issues they will eventually spill over into your dating life.

Being mentally healthy means more than just being able to handle the everyday stresses of life that can come from work, having to be the provider, having to meet expectations, and having to deal with any childhood trauma, among other things. It's about being emotionally resilient and able to maintain healthy, positive relationships.

You've got to be in a place where you're functioning well on your own. If you're not good for you, you're not going to be good for anyone else. We've all seen guys lose it over some minor issue like insecurity, jealousy, or unresolved trauma. Whatever it is, it leads to bad decisions. Don't be that guy.

Women don't want a guy who's mentally all over the place. They want someone who's stable, and mentally healthy. So before you even think about dating, ask yourself: Am I in a good headspace? If the answer is no, take a step back. Work on yourself. Because being mentally healthy and emotionally mature is crucial for success in the dating game.

2. The Financial Side: It's Not All About the Benjamins, But It Kind of Is

Now, let's talk money. This is always the most uncomfortable topic because nobody wants to talk about money, but the truth is, we can't escape it! Whether you like it or not, dating is not free. It costs money. There's no way around it. Whether you're going out for dinner, grabbing drinks, or even just a simple coffee date, you're going to spend some cash. And if you're dating multiple women? Well, you better believe it's going to hit your wallet even harder.

I'm not saying you need to have stacks of money to date, but you do need to be financially responsible and have a steady income. Even I have to admit there have been times I have been dating multiple women, footing the bill, only to realize I was digging a hole for myself financially. If you're struggling to make ends meet, maybe now isn't the best time to dive into the dating scene. There's no point in trying to impress someone with money you don't have. Trust me, that never ends well.

You don't need to be rolling in cash to enjoy yourself or to impress a woman. What you do need is to be smart about it. Even if you're working a minimum-wage job, you can still afford to date if you plan it right. Save up a little, and pick dates that are within your budget. There's nothing worse than going out on a date, trying to ball out, and then realizing you're financially sinking yourself. We call that hustling backward where I'm from.

You better be honest with yourself and with her and act your wage. I've seen too many guys trying to flex by driving a car they can't afford, wearing designer clothes, and taking women to five-star restaurants, only to get hit with credit card debt they can't handle.

Women that are genuine aren't impressed by that stuff. You'll find this out quickly when they keep saying "no" to a second date after you went all out, balling out of control. What this communicates to some women is that you're trying too hard to impress her or you're just trying to get up her skirt, especially if she knows what you do for a living.

The key is to be financially stable within your means. There's a famous comedian who goes by the name TK Kirkland, who doesn't even believe a man should date a woman unless he has 25k in the bank. While I don't agree with that logic, I do get the premise of what he's alluding to. While the average man in America may not have 25k in the bank to date, you should at least be working, have a car, preferably your own place, some nice clothes to wear, etc. If there's anything you should take away from this chapter, I'll say it again, it's that women respect a man who's got his stuff together.

And look, if you're on a budget, that's fine. There are plenty of ways to have great dates without breaking the bank. You don't have to do too much to get the right woman. Women care more about authenticity. I'm specifically speaking to men who try to act the part but don't have it like that. I would rather go on modest dates within my price range that allow me to get to know a person first. I'm trying to keep you from falling into the trap of spending unnecessary money on dates where there is no connection, and ultimately don't pan out.

I want you to understand that dating is an investment. Not just financially, but in time, energy, and emotion. You've got to be smart about where you're putting your resources. Don't blow it all on a gold digger or someone who's just looking for a free meal. Trust me, they're out there. The last thing you want is to be sitting across from a woman who orders the most expensive thing on the menu, pulls out her phone to record a nice meal for views and likes on social media, and then you're sweating bullets when the check comes. GOD forbid your card declines. Be smart. Don't put yourself in that situation.

3. Emotional Control: Don't Be a Loose Cannon

Lastly, let's talk about managing your emotions. Women have started calling men "emotional" more and more, and honestly, we've kind of earned that label. The truth is that men can be just as emotional as women, sometimes even more so. We just show it differently. And sometimes, we don't show it well at all.

I've personally seen and heard way too many examples where a man has let his emotions overtake him. The worst of these examples is physical and verbal abuse. A man should never, and I repeat never put his hands on a woman. I don't care what she does or says to you, there's never a reason to do so. We've seen numerous examples of celebrities and athletes who've lost their cool and thrown their careers away with one bad decision because they couldn't manage their emotions.

You've got to be the guy who stays cool, calm, and collected. Women notice this stuff. They don't want to be with someone who's going to fly off the handle every time something goes wrong.

A real man shows restraint. He knows how to control his emotions and not let them control him. There's an ancient proverb that says, "People with a hot temper do foolish things; wiser people remain calm." Keep that in mind next time you're out on a date and a situation pops up. Maybe the waiter gets the order wrong, or maybe you are out dancing, and someone bumps into you or steps on your shoes. Show her you can diffuse any situation, and be in control.

These are the three pillars that will set you up for success in the dating world. Getting yourself together first. When you've got your foundation solid, you're not just playing the dating game, you're winning it. You'll walk into every date with genuine confidence because you're not going out of your way to impress her but being your authentic self. Nothing is worse than having to try and be someone you're not.

And if she's mad that you're not renting out a whole theatre for her like they do in the movies, walk out and move on to the next one. You can't enjoy dating if you're worried about your credit card statement or bank account at the end of the month anyway. Anything that puts unnecessary stress on your mental, emotional, and financial health is not worth it. That's the rule.

KEY 2: KEEP IT REAL
(HONESTY)

Believe it or not, honesty goes a long way with a woman. A lot of women place a high value on men who can keep it real with them. They're looking for transparency. They're looking for a guy who doesn't hide behind a front but gives them the straight truth. The best time, to be honest is right from the beginning. That's the phase where you're both getting to know each other, feeling things out, and setting the stage. Put all your cards on the table from day one.

One of the biggest complaints I've heard from women over the years is how much they hate being lied to. I've lost count of the times a woman has said, "If he had just been honest with me, maybe I still would've dealt with him." Just tell her what it is, and be upfront about what you're looking for. If you're not looking for a relationship, say it. If you're in a relationship or married, just say it. Look, I'm not the moral police— if you want a side piece, that's your decision— but be real about it. It's that simple. Women don't need every little detail about your life upfront, but they need the truth. No one wants to waste time thinking it's one thing when it's really something else. The worst thing you can do is lead her on, pretending you're available when you're not.

Many women view dishonesty as a form of disrespect, as it implies that you do not value their time or feelings enough to be truthful. A lot of men lie about the car they drive, the job they say they have, being married or having a girlfriend, or even how much money they make. Fellas, it's not worth it. Lies have to be covered by more lies, and the cycle just keeps going and perpetuating itself. Soon enough, you'll be in way over your head. Free yourself from the bondage of living a lie. You'll feel much better trust me. Not only is it deceptive, but if you lie to the wrong woman, that could land you in a world of trouble. Women don't play about their feelings. Don't play with fire. Just be real about who you are.

Be upfront. Be honest about your job— at least you have one. Be honest about your relationship status (I'm assuming if you're reading this, you're single, but if not, still be real). Be honest about the car you drive, or even if you don't have a car, just say it. Maybe you still live with family or have a roommate— just be honest. Honesty does two things. One, it weeds out the ones who might judge you for where you're at in life or the things you may not have. Two, it allows you to live your truth without constantly having to cover up a lie or stressing about slipping up. You don't want to be the guy who tries to keep up with everyone else. That's exhausting and too much work. The right woman will appreciate your truth, and who knows, she may even be someone who can help you grow in the areas where you're lacking, but she needs to know the real you first. Honesty creates that opportunity.

For a woman, an authentic guy is a breath of fresh air. Real honesty is one of the cornerstones that can build genuine trust and connection. We're living in a world full of phonies, fake personas, and social media highlight reels. A lot of people are trying to be something they're not. Be yourself! In dating, honesty isn't just about transparency, it's about being real with your intentions. It's about being genuine, being vulnerable, and knowing that the truth will set you apart from all the others. Honesty gives you an edge, in my opinion. If you are secure enough to show up as you really are, it empowers the woman you're trying to connect with to make her own decisions on how serious she wants to be with you or how far she wants to take things with you, knowing she's getting the real you.

At its core, honesty involves genuine communication devoid of deception, half-truths, or intentional omission. I know I have been guilty of leaving out details in the past with women I've dated. One small detail left out can change an entire story. Or even sharing on an as-needed basis. I'm not saying you have to spill it all on the first date, but we know when those moments arise it's time to be truthful. It involves the willingness to share your thoughts, feelings, and experiences openly, creating an environment of vulnerability and authenticity.

I can tell you from experience that one of the best relationships I ever had came out of how honest I was with her. She respected me for keeping it real with her, and we became best friends before anything else. But the moment I started lying, everything went south. Lies chip away at any foundation of trust. If you're building a connection with lies, eventually, it's going to crumble. If you're upfront, however, you're building on something solid. Lies, no matter how small, have a way of snowballing, and the next thing you know, you're in a mess that's impossible to clean up.

Honesty puts you both on the same page and helps build a foundation of trust. The truth is, if you keep it real from the start, she'll respect that. It's rare to meet a man who's upfront without trying to hide behind some image. Be the guy who values honesty from the start. Pride yourself in telling the truth, even if it's hard because it really is. A woman tends to let her guard down when she feels like she can trust you, when you demonstrate honesty in your words and actions, creating a sense of security and reliability while setting the foundation. Conversely, breaches of honesty often lead to fractures in the foundation you're trying to set with her.

I'm a man, so I know firsthand that vulnerability doesn't come easy to us. If anything, it scares us. Sometimes, it's uncomfortable to admit things you feel insecure about. You might worry about being judged or rejected. We've all held back on the full truth at some point. But being honest also means tackling tough conversations head-on. You might have different opinions or past experiences that you're hesitant to share. But that willingness to open up and address any issues is what sets you apart from other men. If you've messed up in the past or have habits you're not proud of, talk about them. Everyone has flaws. Maybe you've struggled with commitment or have baggage from past relationships. Sharing these things, as long as it's appropriate, shows that you're not hiding who you are. Just like in any relationship, honesty goes beyond sharing the good, it includes the hard stuff, too. By talking openly about conflicts, struggles, and unmet needs, you will build a solid foundation with a woman where there are no ugly surprises.

How many times have you been caught in a lie? Let's keep it real here. We've all been there. I've already told you that in my past relationships, I left out details before or painted myself in a better light when I thought it mattered. But guess what? It always caught up to me. Trying to repair the damage from lying requires even more energy than being honest in the first place. If she's forgiving, she might let it slide once, but most women don't forget. Dishonesty is like termites in the foundation of a house. It erodes trust and leads to insecurity and suspicion. Trust me, no good relationship can be built on a foundation of lies. Start how you want to finish. Small lies only snowball, and once trust is broken, it's a long, hard road to rebuild it.

You don't want to be that guy she's questioning every time you tell her something. So my advice is to start with honesty and keep it consistent. Prioritize transparency, and make a conscious effort to value open communication. Create a safe space where both of you feel free to share your truth with one another. Embracing honesty might mean letting your guard down, and yes, it makes you vulnerable. But that's what creates a real connection. When she senses you're not hiding anything, she'll feel safe enough to let her guard down, too. And that's ultimately what you want. She's probably dealt with enough guys who played games, made empty promises, and hid behind lies. Be different. Be the guy who makes her want to stay.

Now, I get it. Being upfront about everything can be intimidating because rejection is a real thing. There's always a chance she won't like what you have to say. But living in your truth is worth it. If she's going to walk away because of your honesty, that's probably for the best. The truth might make you vulnerable, but it'll also set you free from potential headaches. I'm serious, some women can be a real pain in the neck. So if your truth sends her running for the hills then it's good riddance.

Living your truth is something that I stand on. Even if that means losing out on someone that you really like and are attracted to. Keeping it real means no headaches, no cover-ups, and no worrying about slipping up. You've got nothing to hide, so there's nothing to trip over.

KEY 3: WALK LIKE A STAR (CONFIDENCE)

An essential in the dating game, and I mean essential as in you can't succeed without it, is confidence. It's an absolute must that you develop it and wear it. The ladies absolutely love a man who is confident in his approach, his attitude, and how he carries himself overall as we will discuss. Having it or not having it can either make you or break you.

There's a fine line between confidence and cockiness. Don't be cocky. Cockiness is loud and arrogant like you're walking around with a chip on your shoulder, thinking you're better than everyone else. Confidence, on the other hand, is quiet, calm, and subtle but undeniable. It's the kind of energy that doesn't need to be announced— it just *is*.

You may as well not even attempt if you're going to approach a woman timid, and shy. Point blank period. A woman can detect confidence in a man. It's almost like wearing a great-smelling cologne. A woman can smell it when you walk by, but in this case, a woman can sense it. She can feel it. It's an energy you project. Confidence is an attitude. You can almost cut it with a knife.

You've probably noticed that a lot of guys out there are cocky. They think the louder they are, the more attention they get. But guess what? The kind of attention they attract isn't the kind that lasts. Cocky guys might get a woman's attention for a minute, but it's the confident guy who keeps a woman's attention.

Trust me, women can feel the difference, and no woman is interested in a man who lacks confidence. Confidence is magnetic. It's about how you carry yourself, how you speak, and how you present yourself to the world. Even when you're approaching a woman for the first time, that act alone takes confidence, so approach her with a look in your eyes of being self-assured.

Have you ever watched a lion in a nature documentary? There's something about how they move just calm, strong, and fearless. They don't have to roar to remind everyone that they're the king of the jungle. Their presence alone exudes confidence. That's the kind of energy you want to embody when it comes to dating. I want you to see yourself as a lion. When you walk into a room, walk in like you own the place. You're not begging for attention or validation from anyone. You know who you are and what you bring to the table.

One of my favorite examples of this is Denzel Washington. Women love his walk. It's confident, calm, and composed. Watch him in movies like *Training Day* or *American Gangster*, his stride tells you everything you need to know about his character. And guess what? You don't have to be Denzel to pull this off. Start by paying attention to how you carry yourself. Walk with your head held high, back straight, and shoulders back. Own your space. You don't have to be the best-looking guy or the wealthiest or most accomplished. You can still make a woman *feel* your presence from the second you walk into a room.

Walk like Denzel. Like the cameras are watching every step you take, and every move you make. It's about knowing you're that guy in your mind and the type of energy you project when you're self-assured and grounded in your identity as a man.

I know it seems like some men just have it. Like they rolled out of bed with overflowing levels of confidence, but let me tell you, it takes work to get to that place. So, it's not something you're just born with. Sure, some guys seem to have it naturally, but for most of us, it's built over time. You might have been through some tough experiences like rejection or maybe you were nervous about approaching a woman, or you weren't sure if you were coming off too shy or awkward, and that's knocked your confidence down a peg or two. It happens to all of us

Confidence comes from learning, growing, and improving. That's why you're reading this book. Maybe you need to give yourself a pep talk in the mirror every now and then, and that's okay. The point is to keep pushing forward and believe that you *are* a catch. You have to see yourself the way you want the world to see you first. If you've been shortchanging yourself, it's time for an attitude adjustment.

So, like Denzel, the first thing you have to work on is your body language. As I mentioned earlier, you can't be walking around with your shoulders slouched, dragging your feet, and expect a woman to look your way. How you carry yourself communicates a lot about the type of guy you are way before you even open your mouth. It's called non-verbal communication. It's an aurora you create around yourself.

I once walked into a room, and one young lady told another young lady, who I was friends with, that I walked in with a Denzel-like energy. It's how I got the title for this particular chapter. This is what they told me. I knew them of course, but I kept that in mind that women do pay attention to how you carry yourself. Own a room when you walk into it. Whether it's a lounge, bar, nightclub, private party, company party, or even the boardroom. You've got to make your presence known wherever the ladies eyes may be on you.

In the movie, "Scarface," Tony Montana tells Chico that the boss's girlfriend likes him. Chico asks, "How Do You Know?" He replies, "The eyes, Chico; they never lie." With that being said, the next thing you need to do is upgrade your eye contact game. When you talk to a woman, look her in the eyes. Not in a creepy way, but with intention. Eye contact shows you're not afraid to be present in the moment. It's a subtle but powerful way of saying, "I'm confident in who I am." And women notice. They appreciate a man who's not afraid to look them in the eyes and hold that gaze. It shows sincerity and self-assurance. Again, this is another form of non-verbal communication. You can speak without ever saying a word, just by looking at her.

They say the eyes are the window to the soul, and I believe that. When you're having a conversation, look at her like you're really trying to see who she is. While you're looking into her eyes, pay her a compliment and tell her how beautiful her eyes are. Women love compliments. So, while you have eye contact, capitalize on the moment. It builds a connection and shows you're not intimidated by what she's presenting.

Now, let's talk about the flip side of confidence: insecurity. It's the fastest way to ruin any chance you have with a woman. No woman wants to be with an insecure man, That's a massive turnoff. If you're insecure, you're going to push her away faster than you think. If you're always jealous, clingy, or doubting your worth, she's going to pick up on that right away. Insecurity leads to neediness, and neediness is a huge turnoff.

The truth is, insecurity comes from a lack of self-belief. When you're confident, you don't worry about whether she's talking to other guys because you know what you bring to the table. When you know your value, you don't let jealousy or insecurity cloud your judgment. This automatically increases your market value because, to a woman, confidence is one of the most desirable traits a man can have.

Women want a man who knows he's a catch, just like she knows she's a catch. When you're confident, you don't need to play games or act like someone you're not. You're secure in who you are, and women want that.

While confidence is key, you have to make sure it doesn't cross over into cockiness. Women are turned off by men who think they're God's gift to the world. Also, you don't want to lead with your wallet, your job, or your car. Those things are nice, but they shouldn't define you. If anything, they make you come off as a jerk with no substance to you.

Real confidence comes from knowing who you are, not what you own. When you depend on material things to impress a woman, you're coming off as shallow and insecure. Sometimes, men try to overcompensate in other areas to hide shortcomings or deficiencies in others. Sure, nice cars and fancy dinners might catch her attention, but they won't keep her interested if there's no substance behind them.

If you flaunt your money or possessions too much, you're likely to attract the wrong kind of woman. She'll be in it for what you have, not for who you are. And believe me, you don't want that headache. Social media is filled with men flashing money, driving expensive cars, wearing designer clothes, etc. but are really broke. And after money and material things, have nothing else to offer a woman. Don't be that guy.

So, if you're sitting there thinking, "I don't feel confident," don't worry. Confidence isn't something that magically appears one day. It's something you build. Read books such as this one, hit the gym, take up a hobby you're passionate about, and learn to invest in yourself. You'll notice that as you start to improve in different areas of your life, your confidence will grow too. The more work you put into developing yourself into the best version you can be, the more your confidence will grow.

Look, I'm not naïve. I know there are men who use what they have to get women, but you already know the quality of women this gets you. It's not the kind of woman you can trust. She's the woman who's always on the market, looking for men with money, nice cars, and good-paying jobs to fund her lifestyle. You always have to sleep with one eye open because you can't trust her. If you're that man, more power to you, but good luck trying to find a genuine connection.

Real confidence isn't desperate. It's subtle and not loud. It doesn't seek attention. You're secure in yourself. When you step up to talk to a woman, you know you're worthy of her attention. Remember, you don't have to be cocky to make an impression on a woman, all you need is the kind of confidence that speaks for itself.

KEY 4: LOOK GOOD, FEEL GOOD (APPEARANCE)

When a woman first sees you, before you say a single word, she's already sizing you up based on your appearance. So let's talk about it. You'd think having a good physical appearance would be common sense, but you're wrong. Look, no one's expecting you to look like a GQ model every time you walk out the door, but dressing is an essential part of catching any woman's attention.

Being put together says a lot about who you are as a man. It says you take yourself seriously, and people, especially women, will take you seriously, too. Have you ever heard the saying, "Look good, feel good"? There's truth in that. Before anything else, feeling good starts with how you present yourself to the world. Looking good and smelling good gives you that confidence you need, and women love a man who smells good!

We've all heard the adage, "You never get a second chance to make a first impression," right? This is especially important in the dating game. If you want to stand a chance with that woman, you've got to look the part from the first time she lays her eyes on you. Smelling good, looking sharp, and being groomed from head to toe are non-negotiable.

You could be the funniest, most interesting guy in the room, but if you walk up to her looking like you just rolled out of bed or smelled a little funky, none of that will matter. If you've ever been on a date with a woman who had bad breath, you'll know what I'm talking about. Even if her body is banging and everything else checks out, the moment she opens her mouth, you want to run in the opposite direction. Now imagine how she feels seeing a guy for the first time, and his shirt looks like it was chewed up before he put it on, or his hygiene isn't on point.

What I'm trying to say is that women shouldn't be the only ones putting in the effort. If she can spend three hours getting herself ready to meet you, then you can spend the time making sure you're smelling good, your breath is on point, and your skin is moisturized.

First impressions stick and women notice everything. Seriously, everything. Your shoes, your nails, even your posture. If something's off, they'll catch it. If you're not getting that second or third date or even a first, then start looking at how you're putting yourself together.

Look, it doesn't matter how tall, short, big, or small you are. If your style is not on point, and your hygiene is off, you're already fighting a losing battle. Women are generally more understanding, so they can overlook some things, but being a bad dresser and having poor hygiene are generally things they can't overlook.

Alright, let's get one thing straight— style is subjective. Keeping yourself sharp, crisp, and clean at all times doesn't necessarily mean you have to be on top of all the latest trends. I'm not here to tell you how to dress. However, there are some guidelines you'll want to keep in mind, especially when you're dating. It's not just about the clothes you wear but how they fit. If they're too big? You'll look sloppy. Too small? You'll look like you're trying too hard. Neither is a good look.

You don't have to overthink it, though. Keep it simple. For a casual date, you can't go wrong with a nice pair of jeans and a well-fitted polo or button-down shirt. And please, for the love of all that's holy, leave the shorts and tank tops at home unless you're hitting the beach or a pool party. I get it; you want to be comfortable, but a first date is not the time to show up like you're heading to an outdoor event. Save the laid-back look for later. On that first date, aim for something casual but neat. This means no slides or sandals.

A first date isn't the time to be whipping out your toes. You have to look like you at least put in some effort and slides or sandals don't equal effort.

Believe me when I say that no woman will take you seriously if you don't dress the part. And I'm not joking when I tell you to make sure your shoes fit the occasion as well. Women notice shoes like you wouldn't believe. If your shoes are worn out or scuffed up, it's a no-go. Invest in a good pair of casual shoes or boots. You don't have to break the bank, but your footwear should match the occasion.

Okay, so let's summarize this. If you're going to a restaurant, keep your outfit smart-casual. This means dress it up a little, but definitely not a double-breasted tuxedo. A nice pair of jeans, a collared shirt, or even a good pullover should do the trick. If it's a T-shirt, make sure it's not just a plain white one. Some upscale restaurants won't even let you in if you show up in just a t-shirt. Also, a great tip to remember about t-shirts is if you throw a blazer over it, your look suddenly goes from casual to smart.

We live in a world where resources are literally at your fingertips. Between Pinterest, YouTube, fashion magazines, and even female friends (who are always more than willing to give advice), you've got no excuse for not knowing how to put yourself together. A quick search will give you tons of ideas, from casual looks to more polished styles. So again, have these three things: a blazer, a neat pair of pants, and a good pair of dress shoes.

Let's shift gears for a moment and shift to the hygiene part. You'd think this is common sense, but just to be clear— shower before your date. Yes, this needs to be said. Don't show up straight from the gym or after a long day at work without freshening up. One of the easiest ways to make a good impression is to smell good. If you've ever had a woman lean in and sniff you because you smell too damn good, you'll know what I'm talking about. Now, this doesn't mean you should drown yourself in cologne. Don't go overboard. You're aiming for subtle, not suffocating. A couple of spritzes in the right spots— wrists, neck, behind the ears— are all you need. If she can smell you from across the room, you've gone too far.

So, if there's one thing you should splurge on it's a good cologne. It's one of the best investments you can make in yourself. Again, I'm not saying spend your rent money just to get the best cologne on the market. Plan for it and make sure you get a good one that you can afford. A good bottle of cologne will easily cost a minimum of $100 and can go as high as $400. It's an investment in yourself, and if you're not taking a bath in it, it can last you up to 6 months or even longer.

Next up, your haircut. A fresh cut gives you that polished look, and whether you're going for a clean shave, a fade, or keeping your hair long, make sure it's neat. If you have long hair, make sure even your hair smells good. I've heard stories of women saying how they've dated men with long hairstyles and their hair didn't smell good. So if that's how you roll, make sure you wash your hair regularly. If not, your barber should be one of your best friends by now. I personally get a haircut every week. It keeps me feeling fresh and looking my best. If you have facial hair, keep it groomed. A scruffy, unkempt beard may work for some guys, but not if you're trying to impress on a date. Keep it lined up, neat, and soft.

And while we're on the subject of grooming, let's talk about hands. Yes, your hands. Women notice them. If you've got dirty, untrimmed nails, you might as well kiss that date goodbye. Trust me on this. There's no shame in getting a manicure or pedicure. It doesn't make you less of a man. If anything, it makes you a guy who cares about the details. Some women notice your hands right away, and if they're looking rough or your nails are dirty, that's a turn-off. I don't care how good your game is, if your hands look like you've been digging trenches all day, you're not getting that second date. Plus, keeping your nails trimmed and clean is just a good hygiene habit in general. So, get yourself into the routine of hitting up the nail salon every two or three weeks.

Oral hygiene is another non-negotiable. I mentioned this earlier, but I'm going to tell you again: bad breath is an instant dealbreaker. So before you head out, make sure your teeth are brushed and flossed and you've got a mint on hand. If you're not already, visit the dentist regularly. No woman wants to kiss a guy with bad teeth or funky breath. You want her thinking about how great you are, not wondering why you didn't pop a mint. Good oral hygiene is also part of setting the right impression with a woman and a sure way to land a second date.

Lastly, please, I'm begging you, moisturize. There's nothing worse than shaking a woman's hand and she pulls away because it feels like she's just rubbed against sandpaper. You don't need to invest in expensive skincare, but having soft, well-moisturized skin says a lot about how well you take care of yourself. Ashy, dry, cracked, rough skin will chase all women away. And I mean ALL.

Women love a man who has smooth skin, especially if you work a tough job that's rough on your hands. It's these small details that will set you apart from Joe Blow. And listen, this doesn't mean you need to start hoarding skincare products. Just find a moisturizer that works for you and apply it regularly, especially if you naturally have dry skin.

All these small things, when combined, make a big difference. A well-groomed, well-dressed man exudes confidence without saying a word. And that's attractive to women. When you put effort into your appearance, it shows that you care about yourself and that you're taking this date, this moment, seriously. If she can see that you're taking your date seriously, she will take *you* seriously.

So the next time you're getting ready for a date, check yourself in the mirror. Are you on point? Is your outfit sharp? Are you groomed and smelling good? Don't cut corners. Your appearance does a lot of the talking for you. It not only dramatically increases your chances of having a meaningful conversation, but it also improves the caliber of women you get to choose from in the dating pool.

KEY 5: TREAT HER LIKE A LADY (CHIVALRY)

The famed legendary Motown group The Temptations had a hit song, titled "Treat Her Like A Lady." There's a line in the song that says, "A woman's like a flower, love on her you shower." They go on to reference other points made in this chapter. That brings me to chivalry. By definition, it refers to very polite, honest, and kind behavior, especially by men toward women. Simply put, it's about knowing how to treat a woman. Treating a woman with care, courtesy, and respect shows that you're someone who values her as a *person*, not just as a potential romantic partner.

I was raised with old-school values, which shaped my understanding of how a man should treat a woman. Back in my day, we wouldn't even let a woman pump her gas. If a lady was in your presence, you made sure she was taken care of. Today, though, I see men sitting in the passenger seat while the woman gets out of the car to pump gas, and honestly, it baffles me. Just because times have changed doesn't mean we should forget the basics of treating a woman with chivalry.

This isn't about putting women on a pedestal or taking away from the fight for equal rights— far from it. Women have fought long and hard for equality in many areas of life, and they rightfully deserve the respect and opportunities that come with that. But treating a woman with kindness, politeness, and thoughtfulness doesn't detract from her independence or strength. It only shows that you recognize her value and want to honor it in the way you interact with her.

I'll say that again. Treating a woman with respect, kindness, and gentleness should be the norm. Over time, this way of thinking has been lost with each passing generation. It's a lost art. I don't want to stand on my soapbox here, but I believe many men have gotten away from it. If you can be the one who still values how to treat a woman, you'll stand out from the rest in this day and age. You'll win by treating her with these values because it has become rare.

Unfortunately, in some circles today, we've gone in the opposite direction. We've started to celebrate degrading women, objectifying them rather than building them up or holding them in high regard. Men often seem to forget that kindness doesn't make you less of a man, it makes you a better one.

Some of the gestures I'll talk about in this chapter might seem small or insignificant, but they carry weight, especially in today's world. So we have to get back to the basics of how we should treat the women in our lives. If you can adopt these values, you'll stand out from all the other men, guaranteed. And by the way, it takes nothing from you as a man, to treat a woman well. Nothing.

So, we're going to talk about how to treat a woman right because the fact of the matter is, some of you were never taught how to treat a woman, and you've been fumbling the dating game because you don't know any better.

Let's start with the basics of chivalry.

To explain this better, I'm going to give you a scenario, and we're going to work through the basics of chivalry by addressing different aspects of this date.

Scenario: A woman has agreed to go out on a date with you and she wants you to pick her up at her place.

First things first, be on time. Yes, women take longer to get ready than we do, but rather be on time than keep her waiting. Then, when you arrive at her place, don't sit in your car and more importantly, never, ever, ever honk your horn. That date will be over before it even begins.

The right thing to do is be a gentleman and text or call her to let her know you're outside, then get out of the car and open the door for her. If she happens to live in a building that has stairs, go over and hold your hand out to help her down the stairs, especially if she's wearing heels.

Now, when you get to your car, open the door for her. It's such a simple act but one that so many men forget or ignore. Opening a car door, then closing it behind her once she's seated, isn't just polite but shows her that you're willing to go that extra step to ensure she's comfortable. It's small details like this that help create a lasting impression.

A quick side note is if she lives in a part of town that may be sketchy, I always suggest having her meet you where your date is. Some neighborhoods don't take kindly to unfamiliar faces, so don't try to be a hero unnecessarily.

Making a good impression isn't just for her. You know women talk. When she gets home, she calls up her friends, her sisters, and maybe even her Mom, telling them all about the "wonderful" guy she went on a date with who opened the door for her because men hardly do that anymore. These important female figures in her life will be the ones encouraging her to go on another date with you, even if she has a few doubts.

So, back to the basics. Now, you're at the restaurant. Upon entering the restaurant, you open and hold the door for her again. Minor details, but they go a long way. When you walk into the restaurant or bar, pull out her chair for her and let her sit first. This is classic chivalry at its finest. It's one of those timeless gestures women appreciate.

These little acts of kindness improve a woman's perception of you. All women want to be with men who are kind and sweet to them, and when you do such things for them, they feel respected and cared for. This behavior proves to her that you're the kind of guy who knows how to treat a lady.

You should carry this out throughout the date. For example, when the waiter comes over, always let her order first. This might seem insignificant, but it shows you're thoughtful and considerate of her. If you're familiar with the menu or know a good dish, offer suggestions based on what you know about her likes or dislikes. It's not about trying to impress her with your knowledge, but rather showing her that you've been paying attention and care about her preferences.

Now, let's say the night went well, y'all had a great time, and then the waiter shows up with the check. Under no circumstances ever should you allow a woman to pay on a first date. I strongly believe men should pay on the first date, especially if you were the one who asked her out.

Why would you pursue a woman and then ask her to split the bill when she finally gives you the opportunity to take her out? If you're guilty of this, shame on you. And if you're a woman reading this who's paid on a first date or went half, shame on you too. Even if she reaches for her purse, you stop her and pay the check. Either give the waiter your credit card or slide your bills in before she gets a chance to. Even if she insists, you stop her and tell her it's your treat and you enjoyed spending time with her.

I personally don't recommend going Dutch on the first date. It sets the wrong tone. While going Dutch may be acceptable down the road, I think the man should take charge and pay to set the tone. In my experience, I almost always pay, but there are occasions when a woman, especially one who is independent, will offer to pay or even take you out after you've gone on several dates.

If a woman keeps insisting on going Dutch, it's either a test, or she doesn't want to feel like she owes you. Believe it or not, some men make a woman feel like they're doing her a favor by taking her out. So, if she won't let you pay no matter how many times you insist, pause and check yourself. Maybe you made her feel a certain way, or maybe the date just didn't go well and you both know it won't work out. Still, I wouldn't recommend letting her pay.

Now, I get that everyone's financial situation is different. If you can't swing a five-star dinner, don't feel pressured to do so. Remember, you shouldn't even be dating if you can't afford to date. We already talked about it in the chapter "Setting the Table." Choose a spot within your budget, but the key is to be thoughtful about where you take her. Maybe she's a fan of casual dining, so you can choose a nice fast-food place, not too casual, like McDonald's, Burger King, or Chick-fil-A. I've got nothing against these establishments, but that's not where you take a lady on a first date. The bottom line is to be open and communicative about what she likes and what works for you.

As the date progresses, continue to be thoughtful. For example, when it's time to leave, and she's putting on her coat, don't just stand there; help her with it. Here's another small, yet important gesture. When you're out walking together, always take the side closest to the street. If you're my age, these may not be new to you, but if you're younger, you may not even know about these small acts of chivalry. This is an old-school move that makes a woman feel protected. Once she starts viewing you as a protector, she'll feel safe around you and want to be around you more often.

All these little acts add up. Too often, as men, we think it's the big things that matter, but more often than not, it's the small gestures that win a woman over. Sometimes we think that women are only impressed by grand gestures— fancy dinners, expensive gifts, or elaborate surprises. But more often than not, it's the little things. It's about consistency, care, and thoughtfulness in the small moments.

When the night comes to an end, and you're dropping her off, ask her if she enjoyed the evening. Offer a hug as a friendly goodbye, but never go in for a kiss unless there is clear chemistry or she signals that she's comfortable with it. Consent is very important. Rushing into any form of physical intimacy can ruin an otherwise great date if she's not comfortable with it yet.

Also, don't just drive off the moment she steps out of the car. Wait until she's safely inside before leaving. Or maybe you're even dropping her off at her car, you should still wait until she gets in. Think of how rude it would be for you to drive off, before making sure she's safe in either scenario. It's another small way to show her that you're looking out for her.

Walking her to the door is another option, but she may or may not feel comfortable with you walking her to the door depending on how early it is in the dating phase. You have to gauge that.

The bottom line is this: chivalry isn't dead, but it has become rare. If you can be the guy who still embodies these values, you'll stand out in today's dating world.

KEY 6: ARETHA FRANKLIN (RESPECT)

The Queen of Soul, Aretha Franklin, put it best in her timeless anthem, "R-E-S-P-E-C-T, find out what it means to me." While respect is a word that gets thrown around a lot, it's often misunderstood or even overlooked, especially in dating. Yet, respect is where it all begins. Without respect, there's no way to build trust, connection, or real interest. And if you're looking to set yourself apart from other guys and make a genuine impression on a woman, it's the one quality you'll want to get right.

A lot of men make the mistake of seeing dates as a checklist: show up, make small talk, pay the bill, and call it a day. But respect is way more than the basics. It's about seeing the woman across from you as her own person and understanding that she is someone who has thoughts, dreams, different ideologies, and different life and cultural experiences. By this, I mean you allow her to be her authentic self without judgment or prejudice.

So when you look at respect as a whole, you see that it shows in the little things, like being on time, and the big things, like respecting her right to express her own opinions even if you don't necessarily agree. There's no need to get into a back-and-forth argument just to prove a point. So you see that it goes beyond just opening doors and picking up the tab it means valuing not just yourself but the woman you're dating.

When a man shows respect to a woman he's dating, it demonstrates his maturity, emotional intelligence, and genuine interest in building a meaningful connection. Respect is not just about following societal norms or adhering to a set of rules. It's about treating the other person with dignity, and consideration.

I'll let you in on a little secret: just because you do all the "right" things that a man should do on a first date, doesn't mean you respect her. Women have a sixth sense or something because they can easily see through the BS. If you're full of it, she'll know and frankly, she'll probably check out because you're wasting her time. Respect her time as much as you respect your own. Starting with something as simple as showing up on time might sound trivial, but it's a huge way to demonstrate respect. Imagine you've made dinner plans for 7 PM, but you roll in at 7:30. Even if it's just a slight delay, it sends a message that her time isn't as valuable as yours.

Respecting her time also means understanding her schedule. If she's a single mom juggling work, family, and other responsibilities, she has limited time to give. Respect her availability by planning dates that fit within her schedule and being understanding if she occasionally needs to reschedule.

Pro Tip: If something does come up, communicate it early. Being proactive shows maturity, thoughtfulness, and, yes, respect.

Women appreciate men who can read social cues and know when to give them space. Respecting her boundaries, whether emotional or physical, is vital in creating a safe, comfortable environment where she feels she can be herself. Imagine you're on a second date, and the night is going well. You think maybe it's the right time to lean in for a kiss. But you hesitate, sensing a bit of tension. Rather than pushing forward, the right thing to do is pause. Respectful restraint is attractive. You have to learn to respect her body and her space. Give her the time she needs to feel comfortable, and in doing so, it shows her that you genuinely value her feelings over your own expectations.

Boundaries also extend to emotional topics. She might not want to dive into deeply personal subjects immediately and that's okay.

Giving her the freedom to open up at her own pace respects her autonomy and comfort level. This means respecting her personal space, her right to make her own decisions, and her ability to set her own pace in the dating phase.

Respect for a woman's body and her choices is non-negotiable. I know it can be tempting if she's dressed a certain way, that we may see that as an invitation, but it's not. Just because a woman dresses provocatively doesn't mean she's inviting any level of intimacy. Making assumptions based on how she looks is a common but disrespectful mistake. A man who understands that "no" truly means "no" and doesn't push or pressure gains her respect and her trust. He respects her right to set boundaries and make decisions about her own body and life.

As I mentioned earlier in this chapter, women appreciate a man who can have a conversation without trying to "win" every disagreement. Respect her right to have her own opinions, and instead of dismissing her views, try to understand them. Active listening is an art form and a mark of respect. When you listen attentively, make eye contact, and give her your full attention.

In today's diverse world, dating often involves meeting women from different cultural or religious backgrounds. Respect includes learning about her culture, appreciating it, and showing understanding if she holds values or traditions different from your own.

If she comes from a background where family is central, respect her desire to keep family close. If her cultural values encourage modesty or certain social behaviors, honor them. Don't push her to go against her beliefs for your convenience. Respectful communication also includes knowing when to back off. If a conversation becomes intense or she feels strongly about a subject, don't force your point of view. A man who respects differences will say, "I see where you're coming from, even if I feel differently. Let's talk more about it when you're ready." This creates a space for open, respectful dialogue.

Look, arguments are bound to happen. It's part of being human. But what you can't do is try to assert your dominance. We live in a misogynistic society, and the last thing you need when trying to get a woman to go on a second date with you is to act like you're the one who's always right. Respect also means taking accountability. If you've said something you shouldn't have or made a mistake, own up to it. Apologize and show her that you're willing to make things right. Women value a man who can take responsibility for his actions and make an effort to understand their perspective. They also value men who don't feel threatened by their ambitions, friendships, or personal goals. Don't feel like you have to be with her every second or control her social life. A confident, respectful man encourages her to pursue her passions, supports her goals, and gives her space to thrive.

Respect her friendships, too. Jealousy and possessiveness are not only unattractive but disrespectful. A woman's social circle is a part of her life, and respecting those connections is extremely important. If she's going out with friends, don't blow up her phone, texting her every few seconds. Instead, show her you trust her by giving her space to enjoy her social time without interruptions.

I'm going to keep repeating certain things, even if I sound like a broken record because you need to understand that even in dating, relationships are built on respect. After all, respect builds trust. In dating, respect isn't a tactic, it's a principle. When you commit to it, you create an experience that she will never ever forget. A woman will keep trying to be around a man who is memorable. By embracing these principles and making a conscious effort to show a woman respect, you can establish a foundation that will not only get you through the door faster but will keep you in the room.

KEY 7: WHY SO SERIOUS (HUMOR)

There's a very interesting saying that I've adopted, "Laugh her right out of her underwear." Now, I know this sounds a little funny, but man, it's so true. Making a woman laugh is probably one of the most underrated things a man can do to connect with a woman.

Have you ever seen a not-so-attractive man with a stunning woman? I'm talking about a perfect ten. You probably scratched your head, wondering how he could land such a gorgeous woman. Well, maybe he's loaded. But chances are, he's got her laughing and has a helluva personality. The truth is that women love a man who can make them laugh. No woman wants to be around a man who's mad at the world and takes himself too seriously. Relax and lighten up.

This chapter is for the men who struggle with this or who haven't thought to show this side of their personality or incorporate it into their dating life. You've been leaving out this key element that could give you that needed edge in your dating life and journey.

Now, before we get any further, I need to make it clear that humor isn't just about telling jokes. Don't become a stand-up comedian every time you're around a woman. That's damn near too much. So, it's not just about telling jokes but about showing that you're confident enough to be a little goofy. You don't need to put up a front or be "too cool for school" to impress a woman. For some men, the idea of being funny feels like it might make them look silly or weak— maybe even less masculine. But that's far from the truth. Women find it irresistible when a man can break down those walls and let himself laugh, make her laugh, and not worry too much about how he looks doing it.

I don't know about you, but it's hard for me to be with someone who doesn't have a level of silliness that matches mine. I love sending funny memes and funny videos and finding the humor in things. You should take that same approach with a woman. Someone who doesn't have a sense of humor is like a chalkboard to me. Just boring. Don't be the man who doesn't know how to laugh and not make her laugh.

Countless times, I've heard women say, "He didn't make me laugh" or "He was too serious." Even the Bible says that laughter is medicine for the soul. A good sense of humor can go a long way and even make up for other areas where you may be lacking. Think about it. You can't be unattractive and not funny. You can't be unemployed and not funny. Not to put anyone down, but a sense of humor is a massive plus, no matter who you are.

There's a reason many first dates take place at comedy shows. If you know she's into comedy, why not plan a date around it? Going to a comedy show or a comedy movie is an underrated date idea that could bring you both closer. Comedy shows have the advantage of giving you both a chance to laugh together, which immediately makes the date feel more relaxed and fun. You get to see each other's reactions, and that's where some magic can happen. After all, seeing what someone finds funny can be revealing. It tells you about their personality, their perspective, and their comfort level with certain topics.

And don't underestimate the power of a good comedy movie. It's the perfect setup for a relaxed, lighthearted date where you don't have to do all the talking. Just by laughing alongside each other, you'll naturally feel closer, and you'll have plenty to talk about afterward.

Humor breaks the ice and eases anxiety, which can make the dating stage feel more natural and enjoyable. Leave the overly macho, tough-guy act at home. Life's already tough enough with all the responsibilities we have. When you show a woman that you can laugh and lighten up, it sets a positive tone. A little laughter can completely change the energy. If she's used to guys who are always too serious or focused on impressing her, you'll be a breath of fresh air.

Scientifically speaking, laughter releases endorphins which, as you may know, are commonly referred to as the "feel good" hormones. Endorphins are also released when you have sex. So, put two and two together. Like sex, laughter enhances the bond between two people. It's science! So, laugh a little, bond a little. That's how humor brings you and that woman closer, creating a foundation for a deeper connection. If you asked most women, I'm sure they'd say they prefer a man who knows how to make them laugh over a guy who doesn't know how to make them laugh, who's all serious all the time.

I've met a lot of men who try to act like they've got it all together when they meet a woman, and in the end, she always rejects a second date with them because they are "too stiff." And when I'd ask these guys why they couldn't relax and lighten up, they almost always said they didn't want to embarrass themselves. Now I'm here to tell you, you actually have to lean into that embarrassment a little. You can do this by simply sharing an embarrassing story that you can both laugh over. Sharing these moments can turn an awkward silence into a bonding moment. You're giving her a glimpse of who you are beneath the surface, and that makes you approachable and relatable.

This doesn't mean you should open with an embarrassing story the second you meet your date. Go with the flow of the date and work in a story or two because this will make her share one in turn and keep the conversation flowing.

On a first date, nerves can get the best of anyone. Humor is your best tool for breaking through that initial awkwardness. Instead of starting with the typical "Where do you work?" and "What do you do?" Try something a little different. Lighten the mood with a playful or funny question. For example, one question I've used is, "If you could be a car, what kind of car would you be and why?" It might catch her off guard in a good way and get her thinking creatively. A funny, unexpected question can lead to stories, laughter, and a great icebreaker that shifts the energy from stiff to playful.

If you're nervous, share that too. You could say something like, "I'll be honest, I was a little nervous before coming here. I feel like I just crammed for a test and then forgot everything as soon as I sat down." You're owning your nerves, but in a humorous way, which makes it easier for her to relax and maybe even relate.

Have you ever been around someone who feels like a dark cloud? They complain, have nothing good to say, and generally bring the vibe down. I call them vibe killers. People who don't laugh or know how to have fun can drain the energy out of a room. Don't be the vibe kill. Women are often looking for someone who makes them feel good, brings positivity, and lifts their spirits. Be the guy who adds to her happiness, not the one who brings her down.

Your body language plays a huge role in how your humor is received too. If you sit there with a stiff posture and a deadpan expression, even the funniest comment might fall flat. Be expressive with your face, use your hands to gesture, and don't be afraid to lean in when you're telling a story. Smiling and laughing with her signals that you're genuinely having a good time and enjoying her company.

If she makes a funny comment, don't just brush it off or change the subject. Laugh along, and show her you appreciate her sense of humor, too. There are even funny memes now where men are laughing at a woman's stories in an over-the-top way just to score some brownie points. It's hilarious. The more she feels she can make you laugh, the closer she'll feel to you.

So, let's say you just had a date and the two of you laughed all evening and even scheduled a second date. This is where most men miss the mark. You have to keep the spark alive between that first and second date. Meaning, you have to keep reminding her of the great time she had with you so she'll look forward to seeing you again.

You can do this by engaging in playful banter. This can be done in person, on a call, or even via text. In other words, keep building the chemistry by keeping her laughing and feeling good. Simple, flirty, and lighthearted banter adds a playful twist to the conversation.

Think about the last few dates you've been on. How many of them felt like interviews, filled with the usual "What do you do?" and "Where are you from?" There's a reason dates sometimes feel like a job interview. It's because people are afraid to show their true selves and take themselves too seriously. But from this very moment, you have an opportunity to stand out. Instead of approaching dates like a serious examination of compatibility, take on the "Why So Serious?" mentality. Bring the energy that shows you're here to enjoy the moment. It's contagious, and she'll feel at ease because you're making the experience enjoyable.

While having a sense of humor is essential, knowing when to switch gears is equally important. You don't want to be the guy who cracks jokes during a serious moment or who can't hold a meaningful conversation, so pay attention to her verbal and physical cues. A sense of humor is more powerful when paired with the ability to show empathy and engage in deeper discussions when needed. If she's sharing something vulnerable, that's your cue to dial down the humor and listen intently. The combination of humor and depth makes for a much stronger connection because she'll see that you're a well-rounded man who is able to make her laugh but also able to support her when she needs it.

Have you observed couples who have been together for a while? You'll notice that they often laugh together. Humor isn't just a good strategy for getting her attention, it's the glue that can lead to more dates and her wanting to see you more. Being able to laugh with your date(s) is a powerful bonding tool. It helps you both to lighten things up and not take things too seriously, allowing you to enjoy the experience of getting to know each other in a fun way.

So, go ahead and laugh a little. Lighten up, take a breath, and embrace the "Why So Serious?" approach. Not only will it make dating easier, but it'll also make your time with her more memorable. And who knows, with a good sense of humor, you might laugh her underwear off and your way into her heart.

KEY 8: I'M ALL EARS (A GOOD LISTENER)

There are many universal truths about women, but one of the most important ones is that women love a man who listens. Fellas, you've got to learn how to listen. I'm old enough to remember the old brokerage firm EF Hutton's slogan, "When EF Hutton talks, people listen." I'm not talking about that, "I'm listening because you're telling me what to do" kind of way. I'm talking about actually caring about what a woman has to say. When she speaks, you're locked in, fully present, and attentive.

Now, I know you've probably heard stories about women who've cheated, and a lot of times, those stories start with something as simple as being ignored by their partner. No, that doesn't make cheating okay, don't get me wrong. I'm trying to help you understand just how much being seen and heard means to a woman's psyche, that she'd be willing to go to the extent of cheating from not being heard.

Women need to feel heard, and when we listen to them, we make them feel like we care. When you truly listen to a woman, you're communicating to her that her voice is important to you and that you respect her enough to give her your full attention. When you come off as dismissive or uninterested in the things she has to say, it can become a turn-off. Yes, that means you're not even getting past first base.

Listening is something you have to establish in the early stages of dating when you're learning about her. This is an underrated quality that usually flies under the radar because men are natural problem-solvers. We're naturally wired to fix things. I promise you, sometimes she just needs you to shut up and listen. Let her talk. Let her vent. Just be there. Do you know how many great connections started because a man simply listened to her? No matter what it was.

When you jump in with your advice, solutions, and opinions, you risk cutting off the emotional connection, which is the opposite of what you should be doing. When a woman wants your advice, she will ask you. Maybe if you've been married 10 years and understand who she is inside and out, then you'll know when to offer your two cents, but if it's a first, second, or third date, your job is to listen.

Let me give you an example. Let's say you've been dating a woman for a couple of weeks and she tells you she had a bad day. She's not coming to you to give her a 10-point lecture on what she could have done right or a Ted Talk about how she should change her perspective. If she's telling you she had a bad day, she needs a safe space. But then you take it a step further. Maybe you send her a little pick-me-up text or plan something to brighten her mood like buying her flowers or taking her out to dinner. When she's feeling a little better, ask her how the situation she told you about affects her, and when she tells you, comfort her. The point is to show her that you care about the things she cares about, but more importantly, that you care about *her* feelings.

You know what's crazy? Too many men can completely mess up a date because they don't know when to stop talking. I'm talking about spilling all their secrets, sharing every little aspect of their lives, including the stuff no one should ever know about, and then wondering why she doesn't want a second date.

Sometimes, the less you talk, the better things go. Ever heard the saying, "Loose lips sink ships?" Well, in this case, they might sink your chances with her. There's a time to speak and a time to listen, and you've got to know the difference. If you're always dominating the conversation, trying to impress her with your stories or accomplishments, you're missing the point. She's not looking for you to perform, she's looking for you to connect.

If, for example, a woman tells you about a promotion she's going after, you don't respond by telling her how you got your own promotion. No, you circle back and ask her how it's going. Don't make it about you. Allow her to have the floor and show genuine interest in the things that she has going on in her life. Surprise her by bringing up past conversations you may have had with her about her career, her kids if she has them, her family, and whatever else as it relates to her. She'll be flattered that you cared enough to remember and ask all because you listened.

Men tend to have a short attention span. We want things quick and straight to the point, except in the bedroom, but we'll talk about that in a minute. Men don't like wasting time. It's just not in our nature. We give all the necessary information as briefly as possible and move on to the next thing. It's like rewatching a movie. You already know what the ending will be and you just want to get there. But dating requires more patience than that. It requires you to sit through that whole movie all over again and allow your woman to feel all the emotions of every scene without judging her.

To put this into perspective, imagine you've now been dating the same woman for five weeks and she has a "no sex until the fifth" date kind of rule. Now it's the fifth date and you know there's going to be a happy ending at the end of the night, but because you've been waiting for this day for weeks, you get ahead of yourself and try to skip to dessert when she's trying to have dinner first. Just be patient and learn to just be in the moment.

When you're with her, find out what excites her. What are her dreams, her goals? What makes her laugh, or cry? Ask about her favorite hobbies or the places she's always wanted to visit. And don't underestimate the power of simple questions. "How was your day?" "How are you feeling?"

A very important aspect of genuinely listening is body language. A woman knows you're not truly listening if she's asking you something and you're distracted by your phone or the game that's playing on the TV behind her. Your body has to engage with her. Making eye contact, smiling, leaning in, touching her hand, etc.

So, when you're on a date, keep your phone away. Seriously. Turn it off or put it on silent. You can check the score of the game after the date. When you're with her, she's the only one you see.

I can't tell you how many times I've watched couples on dates, and the guy is glued to his phone while the woman is sitting right there, trying to engage. If you want to show her you're into her, give her your full attention. Look her in the eyes. Ask her how she's really doing. Trust me, she'll notice.

So, let's talk about physical intimacy for a second. Why do so many men strike out with a woman they're interested in? That's because so many men don't understand that listening actually extends to physical intimacy. How will you know she's ready to take things to the next level if you're distracted when she's speaking? Her words hold the key to her boundaries. She will let you know what she wants/needs, how far she's willing to go with you, and what she expects.

Remember earlier when I mentioned the example of the woman with the "no sex until the fifth date rule"? Let's use her as an example again. This woman would have communicated this rule to you either while you were still texting, or on your first date. This rule is not a suggestion. This means you're not trying to cross that boundary on the third date just because you're having a great time unless she *specifically* tells you she's ready for that. However, don't expect her to change her mind; rather, take her at her word and show her that you value her.

A lot of times, women are handing us the answers to the test if we just pay attention. Who doesn't want the cheat sheet, right? And it's not just about big topics like physical intimacy. Even when she talks about the things that went wrong in her past relationships, pay attention. If she says her ex never complimented her, guess what? That's your cue. Compliment her. She's giving you the playbook on what she needs and wants. You just have to tune in and pay attention.

Here's the bottom line. When you listen, you open a door straight to her heart. GOD gave us two ears and one mouth for a reason. You should be listening more than you speak because no matter what a woman's love language is, she wants to feel seen and heard more than anything else. So, be present. Be there. Give her the attention she deserves, and I guarantee you'll see a difference in how she responds to you.

KEY 9: TAKE CONTROL (PLANNING)

A lot of the women I've spoken to seem to have the same energy of "No man is gonna control me." And honestly, I get it. Too many guys out here think that taking control means acting like some tyrannical dictator in the relationship, thinking that's what it takes to be a "real man." They think it means pushing her around, calling all the shots, and flexing so they look tough. That's not taking control. That's just insecurity dressed up as confidence. Real control looks like making plans, putting effort into the details, and leading with confidence so she knows she's with someone who's got it together.

I've been on all kinds of dates over the years and I can tell you that I made sure to tailor each date to whatever the woman was into. The key is to gauge what she might like through your conversations. When it comes to dating, taking control means putting her at ease by planning those first few dates. Women are attracted to men who know how to lead, who make decisions without constantly asking, "What do you want to do?" or "Where should we go?" That's a fast track to nowhere. You asked her out, she's already said yes, so set the tone by showing her a good time. Planning dates, even inexpensive ones, shows that you are making an effort to make your date feel special, valued, and thought about, even when she is not physically present.

The truth is that women appreciate effort. It doesn't have to be a five-star dinner or an all-out adventure (in fact, don't go there right away), but it does need to show you put thought into it. You don't need to overthink it. Just pick something you think she'd enjoy and run with it. You're trying to show her that being with you means experiencing something worthwhile.

I can't tell you how many times I've heard, "You plan something," or "You asked me out." Women get tired of guys who can't make a call. So here's your rule: when you ask her out, already know where you're going and when. Give her something to look forward to. Let her focus on the fun, not on figuring out the logistics. If you're the one to make the plans, she'll take notice that you're not afraid to step up, and she'll feel more comfortable because she knows you've got it covered.

Now, for the guys who think they need to impress her right out of the gate with fancy dinners and flashy dates, let me talk to you for a second. You don't need to break the bank to show her a good time, especially on the first few dates. This isn't just advice to save you but also the guy who will likely date that woman after you. If you keep going all out, blowing all your cash on super luxurious dates, it sets a precedent. Now, the next man who comes along thinking all he has to do is take charge and plan a great date will be at a disadvantage because the woman will expect the sun, moon, and stars from him.

As I said, you don't need to go over the top just to make a good impression. In fact, overdoing it can work against you too. After getting to know her, and you feel there's a connection and vibe, you could plan more elaborate outings and dates. A four or five-star restaurant, more upscale bars, lounges, etc. but make sure to save those upscale spots for when you're further down the line. You don't want to be "that guy" dropping cash like it's going out of style without knowing if there's a real connection. Save the five-star restaurants, concert tickets, and exclusive spots for when you know she's worth it. Set the bar too high on day one, and you might just set yourself up to compete with that same standard every time.

If you don't believe me, ask a woman close to you, a sister, friend, cousin, whatever, ask her what her dating experience was with a man who took her to a five-star restaurant on the first date. Ask her what her expectation was for the second date and you'll quickly learn how women think. When you start something, you've got to finish it. So if you pick her up in a Range Rover for your first date and then on the next date y'all are taking the bus, she's probably going to run far, far away in the opposite direction of wherever the hell you are.

So, take charge by setting the standard from the get-go. You set the standard of what you can afford so she knows what to expect. If you ask me, I think switching up on someone is a form of catfishing. Imagine you see a gorgeous woman on a dating app, you swipe right on her, and you start talking, maybe even FaceTime, and you think she's a ten. Fast forward to your first date, she gets out of the car and you go "Whoa" and find out she looks nothing like her pictures, but now you're invested. That's how a woman feels when you set one standard, and then switch it up once she's invested.

You don't have to do the most. You'll find that the most memorable dates are the simple ones because they're intimate and genuine. If she sees that you've put thought into planning, she'll appreciate it more than an expensive dinner. Women tend to notice thoughtful gestures, and many will make a mental note of the effort you put in. Whether it's a cozy coffee shop, a local bar, a casual dinner, or an activity like mini-golf, these settings let you connect without pressure. When you get a feel for what she enjoys, you can step up to more elaborate dates down the line. Remember, it's not about where you are but how you engage with her.

There's an old saying that goes, "If you fail to plan, you plan to fail." In other words, make sure to take care of the small details too. I'm talking about stuff like making a reservation if you need one, showing up on time, and having a backup plan in case things change. For example, if you plan an outdoor date and it suddenly starts raining, you need to have a backup option. That way, you're never caught off guard, and you maintain that sense of being in control, which reassures her that she's with someone who can handle changes without breaking a sweat.

A "real" man is a man who steps up to the plate. A "real" man is a man who takes control and takes care of his woman in any situation. So when you're on that first date and she's cold, you're taking off your jacket and wrapping it around her shoulders. You're making sure she's comfortable and having a good time. You're making sure she gets home safely even if you're not giving her a ride home. By now, I think you know where I'm going with this because it's one of the themes in every chapter, and that is the *intention* or the "small details."

The small details are also the little things that can put a smile on her face. Maybe you pick up a single rose before you meet her or end the date with a genuine compliment about how you appreciated her company. It doesn't have to be exactly this, but any simple gestures that show you're paying attention to her and that you're invested in the time you're spending together. If the vibe is right, and the date went well, let her know you'd like to see her again. Don't wait around, wondering if she's interested, be upfront. Thank her for coming out with you, and if you had a good time, mention wanting to set up something else soon. What you should never, ever do is play those childish games of waiting three days to get back to her.

That "three-day rule" might make for a good rom-com plot, but in reality, it often just creates unnecessary tension and confusion. Women appreciate clarity and honesty. If you had a good time, let her know! There's no need to overthink it. A simple, sincere follow-up shows her you're both intentional and interested, which is a rare but appreciated quality. So you better leave those rookie games behind and don't confuse a woman, making her wonder whether you like her or not. If you want to keep seeing her, let her know, plain and simple.

The more effort you put in now, the more she'll see you as someone who's worth her time and attention. After all, a woman wants a man who knows how to take control, not just for one date, but as someone she can count on. So, plan it out, own it, and show her what it's like to be with a man who's confident enough to lead.

KEY 10: WEIRD SCIENCE
(KNOW YOUR TYPE)

In the 1985 film *Weird Science*, two socially awkward high school teenage boys sit down with an old computer and "design" their dream girl. They pick everything about her from her body type, personality, and more. In a bizarre series of events, their creation magically comes to life. How ironic that if you fast forward to today, almost 40 years later, while we can't quite conjure our ideal woman out of thin air, technology has made it so that you can "select" the specific type of woman you want to date on dating apps, dating websites, and all kinds of women to choose from on social media. With just a few clicks, you're filtering through hundreds of profiles based on looks, lifestyle, hobbies, and even personality types. Now, why am I bringing this up? Because just like those guys in *Weird Science*, you need to think about the kind of woman you want, and or women you want to date. If you're serious about dating with purpose, defining your "type" is where you need to start.

Being able to zero in on a specific type will help you to narrow down your choices. You can't catch 'em all, or rather, you can't say you want to date them all. That's just a lazy approach and one that's bound to waste your time and leave you spinning your wheels. Getting specific about your type means you're not just casting a line into any waters, you're fishing where the type of fish you actually want are swimming. This should be a part of your dating game plan. So, take a second to think about what she looks like. Is she tall, short, petite, or thick? Is she into fitness, or does she like a more laid-back lifestyle? Does her culture or ethnicity matter to you? Does she have long hair or short hair? Does she work a 9-to-5 or run her own business? Is she a party girl, or is she more of a homebody? Does she smoke or drink? Quick sidebar: I personally like a woman who drinks, especially tequila. So if she drinks, that's a plus in my book. Nothing against a woman who doesn't, but that's my point. Find what works for you. These are all questions you need to ask yourself to help you paint a mental picture of your ideal woman. If you're out in the world looking without knowing what you're looking *for*, you'll keep hitting dead ends or dating women who are wrong for you. So, it's time you stop wandering around, hoping to get lucky.

There are all types of beautiful women in the world. The world is your oyster when it comes to your choice of women. Studies have shown that the number of women outweighs the number of good men out here. So, there's no shortage of women, but there is a shortage of good men. So as men, we have the advantage. Play it to your advantage.

Every man is visual, let's not front. We're visual creatures. A beautiful woman with all the right physical traits can stop you dead in your tracks. It's like everything goes slow-mo when she walks in. She checks all the boxes you've imagined in your mind, and for a split second, you're convinced she's "The One." But looks are only one part of the picture. A beautiful face and a great body can only take you so far if there's no chemistry to back it up. Now if you can get looks and chemistry, you're winning. Having mutual interests, likes, beliefs, desires, goals, etc., are all things that make for great chemistry. I've seen men who date toxic women simply because they're pretty and have a Coke bottle shape for a body but don't have any chemistry. As a man, your peace of mind should outweigh a piece of a**. Sorry to be so blunt, but maybe you're reading this and you're in that situation or know someone in it, and you need to free yourself. Dating shouldn't be full of drama or stress. Some wrongly attribute that kind of toxic attraction to love and connection. The moment you recognize there is no chemistry, and you don't have things in common with a woman, pull the plug. You're saving yourself a headache down the road, trust me. Having things in common with a woman makes for a much more harmonious and fun dynamic. You want a woman who makes your life better, not one who turns it into a soap opera.

To help you get a clearer idea of what's out there, let's break down some of the common types of women out in the world for you to choose from. No, not every woman fits neatly into these categories, but these can give you an idea of the general characteristics and values you might encounter in dating.

First, you have the independent working woman. These women are the breadwinners, the hustlers, the 9-to-5ers who don't need anyone's help to make things happen. They're out there working their way up in their careers, paying their bills, and keeping their lives together. Typically, these women have a strong sense of independence and are used to handling things on their own. Some have a little Alpha in them. They aren't looking for a man to complete them, they're looking for someone who can add value to their lives. If you're into dating someone who's ambitious and has her own career and goals, this is your type. Just know that she's likely going to prioritize her career and might expect you to bring something solid to the table as well.

Then, you have what I call the "social media type" of women. These are the influencers, the IG models, and, yes, even the *OnlyFans* models. Social currency is their game, and they care more about followers, likes, and validation from the internet. If you're interested in a woman like this, just know what you're signing up for. Her social media is part of her brand, so you'll need to get comfortable with her prioritizing her image and likely a lot of attention from other guys. It's not for everyone, but if you can handle it, more power to you. Remember, though, many of these women are drawn to men with a certain economic status, social clout, or cache to add to their status. If you can't bring anything significant to the table and value your privacy then this probably isn't your type.

You also have women who are business owners and entrepreneurs. The entrepreneurial type is self-driven, ambitious, and independent, building her empire. She's passionate about what she does, putting in the hours, and probably making a name for herself. This woman appreciates a man who's equally ambitious and motivated. In other words, she wants a partner who is similarly wired. Someone who understands the late nights, the hustle, the grind. Just like the independent working 9-5 working woman, she's not here for games; her time is precious, and she respects a man who values his own hustle too.

These last two groups of women I described are probably not dating you if you're sitting at home playing video games all day unless you're a streamer getting paid to do it. So if you don't have your ish together, don't even bother trying to get with these women.

The last group I'll talk about is the women who want to be taken care of by a man. They're looking for the come-up. A successful man, athlete, or has a good-paying job. They want their bills paid, allowances, trips, shopping sprees, etc. To these women, men who do all this for them are called "Tricks" or "Sugar Daddy's." Some men knowingly sign up to date in this group of women, because it's more transactional or unknowingly are being taken for a ride.

While I described four different groups of women, some of these women can overlap in each group. For example, an IG model could also be a business owner, and a woman with a 9-5 could also be looking for a Sugar Daddy. Maybe you want to swim in all of them. Maybe you like a woman who's more of a homebody with a 9-5 job. Maybe you don't mind dating an influencer who's also an IG model.

It's all about knowing yourself and what you're comfortable with so you can move accordingly. There's no wrong answer, but whatever type of woman you're drawn to, go in with your eyes open. Define what matters to you, be clear on the kind of dating relationship you're looking for, and don't settle for anything that doesn't fit your vision. You have the freedom to choose, so don't waste it by compromising on things that will end up being deal-breakers down the road. When you know *your* type, you attract the right type. No dating relationship will be completely perfect or stress-free, but knowing what you want, and more importantly, what you *don't* want, will save you a lot of time and energy.

KEY 11: THE R WORD (REJECTION)

I'll start by saying, dust yourself off because if you're reading this, you're already doing better than most guys out there who take a few hits and throw in the towel. Real talk, every guy who's been dating long enough has faced rejection. Anyone who says he hasn't is probably lying, or he hasn't stepped out and tried. At least you've got the guts to go for it. So you shot your shot, and it didn't land even though you went in smooth, with your best lines, looking like a million bucks... and she still turned you down. It sucks, yeah. But it's not the end of the world.

Some of you might be feeling beat down, thinking, *Man, maybe this whole dating thing just isn't for me.* Maybe you've tried over and over, only to get shut down so many times that it's messed with your head. That's why I'm dedicating an entire chapter to rejection. Rejection deserves a deeper dive. Why? Because if we're being honest, no one likes rejection, but for men, it's different. Rejection can hit harder and cut deeper. Men hate it because it messes with our sense of pride, self-worth, and even ego. When you face it, it's easy to feel like you're somehow "not enough." The truth is, rejection isn't about you not being "enough" at all. Yet, a lot of guys take it so personally that they turn hostile. A lot of women get verbally abused, sometimes even physically assaulted, just for not welcoming a man's advances.

Let's stay on this point for a minute because too many men take rejection as a reason to get angry or resentful. We've all seen it happen, guys losing it because a woman didn't respond to them the way they wanted. They go from "Hey, beautiful" to throwing insults in seconds flat. I've even seen dudes get aggressive like they're entitled to a woman's time and attention just because they approached her. I've got a friend who told me about a guy who threw *potato salad* at her because she wouldn't stop and talk to him. Potato salad? How fragile do you have to be to resort to that?

This kind of behavior is extreme, but it highlights something important and that is sometimes, we let rejection mess with us in ways it shouldn't. Physical or verbal abuse towards women is not acceptable, ever. Especially if she just doesn't want to talk to you. It's never that serious, but sometimes as men, our egos can be so fragile mentally and emotionally that rejection cuts to our very core. We can see rejection as a personal attack when it's not personal at all.

If you're finding yourself getting angry, bitter, or taking rejection personally, it's time to step back and ask yourself *why*. Dig a little deeper. Why is it triggering such a reaction? Maybe it's entitlement, maybe it's ego, maybe it's past trauma, maybe it's just the idea that someone doesn't see you the way you want to be seen. Whatever it is, understanding why rejection messes with you is the first step to dealing with it. Every woman is not going to want to talk to you. That's just the way the cookie crumbles. Even the best players miss shots. Steph Curry can drain threes like no one else, but he still has off nights. You're going to miss a few shots, and yeah, sometimes you'll strike out. But like any good hitter in baseball, you've got to keep stepping up to the plate.

If you're struggling with rejection, I want you to re-think your approach to dating and try the "batting .300 principle." In baseball, a .300 batting average is considered great, even though it means striking out 7 out of 10 times. Think about that. Professional baseball players get paid millions to strike out almost every time they go to bat. But most importantly, even though they will inevitably miss a few, they still keep swinging. So, if you approach 10 women and only 3 respond positively, you're batting .300, and that's a solid average. With this mindset, rejection becomes a part of the game rather than a personal failure. It keeps things in perspective as you learn that each "no" brings you closer to a "yes."

I started the book by addressing your mental and emotional state before getting deeper into the dating game for a reason. Rejection is a major part of the game. Even if you're the guy who's got it all, best believe there's still a woman somewhere who will reject you. Like I said, you can't take it personally. There have been women that I was attracted to, that I wanted to go out with, but they wouldn't give me the time of day. You simply just have to move on. Everyone ain't for everybody.

Now that we're on the same page, let's talk about the different ways women curve men. You might not be aware of this yet, but women have their ways of saying "not interested." They might not all look or feel the same, but trust me, they all mean the same thing.

First, there's the flat-out curve. This is when she tells you straight up she's not interested. She's direct, doesn't waste your time, and doesn't dance around it. She's the one that you try to talk to, and she says, "No, thank you, I'm not interested." And while it can be a bit embarrassing, you have to respect it. Don't push it, just accept the L and move on. At least she's clear and honest.

This second one is more for all you online fellas. It's what I call the "DM curve." In this digital age, the ghosting game is strong. She's leaving you on read, not responding to your DMs, or worse, responding with one-word answers. That's a big fat "no." If she's not replying, don't blow up her DMs. No response is a response. It's a big, silent "no thank you." Move on. Don't get creepy, don't hit her up ten more times like a stalker, hoping she'll change her mind. Just let it go unless you enjoy getting blocked.

We also have the third, and somewhat strange way women curve men is the slow curve. This is the one that confuses a lot of guys because it feels like there was something there. You hit it off, maybe exchanged numbers, texted, had a phone conversation or two, or even went on a date or two. And then— poof— she disappears. Your calls go to voicemail, texts go unanswered. You're stuck wondering what happened. Well, either she was using you as a rebound or a distraction while she figured her stuff out with another guy, or she lost interest in you for any number of reasons. Maybe it was timing. It could also just be plain old life getting in the way. People go through things, and sometimes people have to take a step back and focus on themselves. Trust me, it happens. So you take a step back, respect her space, and match her energy. If she circles back, she'll do it. But whatever the case, don't chase a ghost.

No matter how it comes, rejection still sucks, but as I repeat for the umpteenth time, don't make it personal. I have a saying, "It's going to be, what it's going to be." I never worry about things that are out of my control, and how someone responds to me or you is one of them. Whether it is negative or positive. What you can control is your attitude and how you respond. Getting angry, upset, or in your feelings is not how you want to handle it. Don't allow rejection to cause you to do crazy things like become a stalker. Yes, I've heard the stories, and men stalking women who no longer wanna deal with them is a real thing. Remember this nugget, sometimes, when you follow, they flee, but when "YOU" flee, they follow. Let that sink in.

Alright, so how should you handle it when you get shot down? Because you can't just read about this stuff, you've got to put it into practice. The first thing you have to do is pause and process. If you don't do this, you'll get into your feelings quickly and take it personally. Every man has an ego, and rejection bruises that ego and that's when, if left unchecked, things can go left. But we're not doing that around here. Start looking at rejection as a blessing in disguise. Maybe God was saving you from something or maybe the timing was just off. Now, this means you should reflect, but don't dwell on all the possible reasons why she rejected you. I'm not saying you shouldn't introspect, but I'm saying don't overanalyze everything. Have a next-up mentality in the meantime. Meaning that GOD didn't stop making women the last time I checked, so it's on to the next. I talk about this in depth in the chapter called, "Don't Chase, Replace." You have to know that you're a catch too. You have to think of yourself in that light. I want who wants me. You should too. Don't allow rejection to beat you down.

Think of rejection as fuel. Take that hit to the ego and use it to improve yourself. One of the greatest stories of rejection is Michael Jordan to use another sports analogy. Some of you may know the story. He was cut from his high school varsity basketball team, only to be sent down to the JV ranks. Arguably, one of the greatest basketball players ever (depending on your generation) to lace up sneakers and pick up a basketball was told he wasn't good enough. Imagine if he would've quit. He took that hurt and rejection and used it to motivate him. You, too, must do the same. Remind yourself that there's always room to level up. Hit the gym, pick up a new skill, expand your interests, and so on. Become the kind of guy who's worth a second look. You don't always get the woman you want, but sometimes you'll find someone who actually fits your life even better.

There are 4 aces in a deck of 52 cards. Dating can feel like trying to find an ace in a deck of cards. You want the aces. However, you might have to go through a few jokers before you get to the aces. There are plenty of women playing games out there, but what you want is someone who truly values you for who you are as a man. Some of you are wasting your time being the clown in someone's circus. You're better than that.

Sometimes the woman you want isn't even good for you. As long as you know you've done everything in this book, you can be at peace with that. Rejection is like being tackled in football. It's part of the dating game. When a woman doesn't choose you for whatever reason, look at it as her loss, and not yours. And who knows, it could've been a blessing in disguise.

KEY 12: GO FISH (THE CATCH)

Fishing is an art, a skill, and sometimes requires a little bit of luck. Anyone who fishes will tell you that success depends on knowing where to cast your line, how to approach the fish, and what bait to use. Meeting women is a lot like fishing. You need to know the certain places where the fish bite. This means you need to be in the right place with the right "bait" and, most importantly, the right mindset.

As I stated in the introduction, there was a time when there were no things such as social media or dating apps. Today, you don't even have to leave your house to meet women. Technology lets you swipe right and shoot DMs, and even check out a person's background before you even get to meet them and ask questions. But there's something to be said for meeting a woman in person. I'm talking about the kind of connection that happens face-to-face, where attraction is sparked through a smile, a similar sense of humor, or even a sense of style. There's an energy to it, an element of surprise, and, frankly, a bit of an adrenaline rush. And for those of us who enjoy that thrill, "fishing" in the real world is still where it's at.

Sure, I've met my fair share of women on social media and dating apps, but for me, nothing compares to approaching a woman in person. Whether she's at the bar, on a walk around the lake, shopping for groceries, or lifting weights at the gym. In those moments, there's a buzz that kicks in. Think of it like a predator locking in on its prey, ready to make a move. You feel that pressure, that excitement flowing in your veins before you go in for the kill.

Now, before we get into the places where you can meet women, the thing that stops most men before they even try is the fear of rejection, which I discussed in the previous chapter at length. Nobody likes getting turned down, but you have to get comfortable with that feeling because, in this game, rejection comes with the territory. As I mentioned you'll strike out sometimes. You might even strike out a lot. But each time you do, you learn and refine your skills so that you can get that "big catch" later on.

Using the fishing analogy again, if you don't catch anything one day, are you going to quit fishing altogether? Of course not! It just means you might need to try a new bait, change your location, or rethink your approach. Maybe she was taken, maybe you weren't on you're "A" game that day, or maybe you're just not her type.

So now you've got to man up. It's go time. I'm going to break down some of the best places to go fish, along with tips, dos, and don'ts that can make or break your chances. Let's start by talking about three of the most common places men and women meet on a night out. Bars, lounges, and nightclubs.

There's a reason bars, lounges, and nightclubs are tried and true grounds for meeting women. This is because everyone's out to have a good time, the vibe is relaxed, and you have endless opportunities to approach without it being weird. People are also drinking and enjoying cocktails, and drinking alone tends to loosen people up and make them more sociable. However, you need a solid strategy.

First, if you see someone you're interested in, try to make eye contact. A quick glance followed by a smile is often all it takes to show that you're interested without coming on too strong. Making eye contact is a subtle, but yet non-verbal form of communication. It lets her know you see her. Now, when I say eye contact, I don't mean staring creepily. We've talked about this. Don't stare women down like a stalker. Keep it casual, confident, and brief. If she holds your gaze or gives a quick smile, you might just have an open invitation to approach.

But before you even think of taking a step in her direction, assess the situation. Is she with friends, or maybe even a date? Avoid putting yourself in a sticky situation by making a move without checking to see if she's taken. Once you're clear, approach with confidence but keep things light and respectful. And remember this golden rule: Compliment, compliment, compliment! Whether it's her eyes, her smile, or her outfit, a genuine compliment can set the tone for the entire conversation. I recommend you avoid the basic stuff that anyone could say. No, you need to be specific. Women love a man who pays attention. So go in with a compliment that isn't superficial, but also shows that you pay attention to details. For example, if she has dimples or she's naturally pretty, compliment her on those features. Personally, I love naturally beautiful women. So when I see a woman who is out with little to no makeup, I point that out. If you really like her dress, say more than just "nice dress" as this shows her that you're truly paying attention to details. Better yet, go in with humor to break the ice. I'd say, "Girl, you wearing that dress."

Here's a tip: if she's with friends, consider offering to buy a round for her whole group. Not only is it a generous move, but it often wins her friends over, which can work in your favor. Just be aware, though, that not every woman at a bar, lounge, or club is genuinely interested in connecting. Some might just be out for a good time, and there are always a few who know how to finesse a free drink or two. It's part of the territory, so don't take it personally if you encounter it.

Now, let's say you've walked over to her, got her attention, and she seems interested; now what? Keep that initial conversation short and sweet. In other words, don't talk her ear off. Get in and get out. Get straight to the point. It's like the movie Gone in 60

Seconds. I'm also a believer in less is more. Let her know you're interested and ask for her number so you can continue the conversation in a quieter place. But here's a pro hack: give her your number instead, and I'm going to tell you why. It's the quickest way to know if she's interested. If a woman is attracted to you she'll message or call you. I don't always recommend that approach, but it's one to keep in mind. Women, for the most part, like to feel pursued. It's part of the chase. The main thing to remember, however, is that one of you has to give out their number, otherwise it's a bust. Bars and nightclubs are generally loud places, and no one wants to yell over loud music all night.

There are also so many other places. The gym can be a great place to meet women, but you have to tread carefully here. Many women go to the gym to focus on their workouts, so it's crucial to respect their space and avoid interrupting them when they're clearly in the zone. The best approach is subtle and respectful. The gym is a personal space, and nobody likes to feel watched while they're mid-workout. Start slow, see if she's receptive, and always approach with a simple, "Mind if I join you?" or "Need a spot?"

Then there's the grocery store. Yes, you can still meet women at the grocery store. When you spot someone interesting, find a way to make a lighthearted conversation about something if you're in the same aisle, ask for a quick opinion, or comment on the best organic grapefruit juice (I've done it). And let's not overlook coffee shops, airports, churches, and other everyday places. The key in these settings is to approach with a relaxed, respectful attitude. Start with a simple line like, "Excuse me, do you mind if I have a moment of your time?" If she's open to talking, you can follow up with, "Are you married or spoken for?" I like to use spoken for because if you wanna be technical if she's not married, she's single. This question is respectful and direct, letting her know your intentions without being too forward.

I remember one time I was at DFW Airport on a brief layover. A sexy station agent was working for a particular airline I won't mention. I observed her for a minute before making my approach. Finally, I decided to go shoot my shot. That's a mentality within itself. I approached her, complimented her, and proceeded to make light conversation. We hit it off and exchanged numbers. She even took a break, just so that she could walk with me to my departing gate. We still keep in contact at the time of the writing of this book. We hit it off so well, that whenever I fly through DFW on her carrier, I'll let her know, and she'll upgrade my flight to first class. All that because I wasn't scared to open my mouth and go fish. The point of this story is that I can meet a woman and approach her anywhere. If I see someone I'm physically attracted to I approach her. It's as simple as that. As we say, where I'm from, a closed mouth doesn't get fed.

Okay, we've covered some of the most popular places to meet women in person, but what if you're not into the bar, lounge, and nightclub scene? What then? There are still plenty of places to meet women and the most popular place is online. While this is not a book strictly about online dating, it is a place to meet women that has become a hotbed for men to go fish. There's even a popular dating app called Plenty of Fish. Even if you're an "old school" guy who prefers meeting women face-to-face, having a solid online presence can still work in your favor, so let's go over a few things that you have to get right before you start fishing online.

First of all, create a profile that reflects who you truly are. It's tempting to create the perfect profile, but say 'no' to that temptation. Use recent, clear photos where you're looking good but still look like yourself. I've seen guys post pics with exotic animals, shirtless pics, and from the most luxurious places in the world. Don't do that. Keep it simple. Even if you love traveling, having a picture with a koala hanging on your shoulder is overkill. Then you want to write a good bio. List all your activities and create a nice bio that is honest, and to the point. When direct messaging, keep it short and sweet. This is not the place to write long essays.

When you make a connection with a woman, keep your message short and sweet. Start with a light opener or a simple compliment, and avoid sending novels in the first few messages. If she doesn't reply immediately, don't double or triple-text. Instead, let it go and move on. Desperation is a surefire way to kill attraction. There's a fine line between being persistent and coming across as needy, so give her space and allow things to develop naturally.

One way to look at online dating is like fishing in a different pond. There are plenty of fish here, too, so if you're ghosted or ignored, don't let it discourage you, and don't get mad and go off on her. If she's not interested, move on. There's a difference between being consistent and desperate. Consistent is maybe checking in once a week or every two weeks. Not multiple messages every day. Never come off as desperate with a woman.

As I said, in fishing, just like in dating, you're not going to "catch" something every time you cast your line. Sometimes you get a bite; sometimes, you don't. Just keep tweaking your technique, changing your bait, or switching fishing spots until you find what works for you.

KEY 13: TALK A GOOD GAME (COMMUNICATION)

I'll be the first to admit that talking to a woman in a way that engages her isn't always easy. Where I'm from San Francisco, Ca., we call it the "gift of gab." Some guys have it, some don't, but the good news is that communication is a skill that can be learned and perfected. Sure, for some men, walking up to a woman and making her feel like she's the only person in the room comes naturally. A few of my friends have that ability. But some men are terrified of talking to women. A guy once asked me, "How do you do it? How do you just start a conversation with a woman?" I looked at him and said, "By opening your mouth!" It's funny but true. Starting is the hardest part, but the more you do it, the better you become at it.

It sounds simple, but that's the starting point. Just approach, open up, give it a go, and talk to more and more women. In the beginning, you might stumble, or maybe you'll feel awkward. But it's like learning to ride a bike. You'll fall, you'll get scraped up, but once you get the hang of it, you're off to the races.

Has that been your experience? Scared to talk because you don't know what to say? Or maybe you're that guy who just stays quiet because you feel like you won't say the "right" thing? You'd be surprised how many men feel this way. A lot of men are stuck at the gate, afraid to approach the women they're interested in because they're overthinking it.

I've touched on rejection in previous chapters and how it has killed a lot of men's confidence. Maybe you were out one time, saw a gorgeous woman among her group of friends, and decided to shoot your shot, thinking you stood a chance. Maybe you even approached her all respectfully but she came at you crazy. A lot of men have developed a fear of talking to women because they've had experiences like this or worse, but unless you plan on becoming a monk, you're going to have to talk to women to get a woman. To get good at anything, you have to actually do it. So, you've got to start talking to more women.

One of the easiest ways to open a conversation is with a question. Simple as that. Questions are the ultimate icebreakers. They open the door to meaningful conversations and show that you're genuinely interested in her world. Start with something simple. Ask her what she likes to do, where she's traveled, what foods she loves, or what her passions are. Here's another good one: Ask her if she could be a car, what kind of car she would be, and why. Thank me later. That one always gets them and makes them think and have to elaborate. These are natural starting points, things that almost anyone can talk about comfortably. Questions like these make it easy for her to open up, and you'll be surprised at how many conversations flow naturally from just one good question.

Here's a very important tip: ask open-ended questions. If you don't know what that means, these are questions that require more than a "yes" or "no" answer. Like the examples I just gave you above, an open-ended question would be something like, "What's the first thing you do when you wake up?" Even if she gives a one-word, answer like "Read" or "Pray," it gives you something to build off of. If she said, "pray," for instance, you could then follow it up by asking about her beliefs. This means the conversation will keep flowing as long as you keep asking open-ended questions. So, start with a question, pay attention, and show interest in her responses.

Talking to a woman and making a connection involves a little mental and verbal stimulation. Let's call it verbal gymnastics. A lot of men are too nervous to make their intentions clear, and that's where they miss it. Communication isn't just about the words you say but about conveying your purpose, your vision, and what you're looking for. Let's be honest, a closed mouth doesn't get fed.

Too many men are stuck, watching from a distance, nervous to say anything and end up missing out on women they're genuinely interested in. She might be waiting for you to take the first step. So make it clear. If you're into her, if you want to take things to the next level, say it.

A lot of us men are worried about coming off as "too much" or "too forward," but the reality is that many women appreciate when a man can genuinely express himself and his intentions. They are attracted to men who can confidently articulate their thoughts and intentions. I understand that we as men sometimes don't always possess the ability to express ourselves, but you have to get over that. Being able to communicate is one of the qualities that differentiates a boy from a man. A man knows what he wants and isn't afraid to express it.

This is especially important if you're serious about dating her. Be up-front and honest about your intentions. If you're dating with the end goal of a relationship in mind, let her know. If you're just enjoying the moment and seeing where things go, say that, too. A woman will respect you for doing that. It's the men who lie and deceive that most women have a problem with. The best time to be forward and direct is in the beginning.

I'm not going to tell you or advise you to lie to get what you want from a woman. This is not that kind of book. This book is about being your true authentic self. Believe me, some men lie to women to get what they want, and this is no knock against them. I've witnessed and learned over the years that the ability to say what you want goes a long way. Being authentic and real is telling her the truth, and still getting what you want. Women aren't mind readers. As men, we have to let them know what we are thinking and expect. The last thing you want is to mislead her or waste each other's time because you weren't honest upfront.

Remember, communicating isn't just about what you want but also about where you are in life. Let her know if you're working on yourself, growing, or figuring out what you want in life. Women are drawn to men with direction, vision, and purpose, and there's nothing wrong with not being there yet, but you've got to say something. You'll save yourself a lot of wasted time, money, and potential headaches if the two of you aren't on the same page. How many times have we as men been in the cross hairs of a misunderstanding due to not communicating what our intentions are? Be clear, be direct.

Another important nugget when it comes to communication, which I mentioned in an earlier chapter, is giving compliments. Once you get a woman talking it's important to build her up, not tear her down. Don't be condescending or negative. Women get enough of that from the world. They don't need it from the guy they're talking to, especially if that guy is you. If you're condescending and belittle her, things will likely fizzle out fast, and your whole goal and objective is to keep the fire burning. Compliments are a simple yet profound way to express appreciation and admiration for the person you're attracted to or interested in. They can strengthen the emotional bond between you, and the person you're attracted to, create a deeper sense of intimacy, and create a more positive and fulfilling relationship dynamic. Compliment, compliment, compliment! I can't stress this enough. Just like a woman loves gifts, they love compliments, and compliments are free! It cost you nothing to say nice things about the woman you're dating. And why wouldn't you? Make her feel good. She could be anywhere else but she chose to be with you.

Think of complimenting her like taking care of a garden. If you plant seeds, you don't just leave them alone, you water them, nourish them, and give them light so they'll grow. A woman's confidence is similar. Compliments are like that water that nurtures and encourages her to flourish. In the same way, you have to water a woman with compliments. Doesn't take a rocket scientist or farmer to figure that out. Tell her how good she looks, how good she smells, how beautiful her eyes are, how you admire her work ethic, etc. When she gets her hair done, tell her how pretty it looks.

Beyond compliments, share a bit of your vision for life. This can be powerful because, as much as a woman loves compliments, she also loves a man with ambition and a sense of direction. When you share your goals and dreams, you're not only letting her see a deeper side of you, but you're also showing her that you're a man with purpose. Talk to her about where you see yourself in the future, what drives you, and the things you're passionate about achieving. This gives her insight into your values and lets her imagine what being with you might look like.

So, here's what you need to remember: open your mouth, be honest, ask questions, listen closely, and, of course, don't forget to compliment. Talk that talk with confidence and intention. You don't need to have all the right words, you just need to be real. Let her see you for who you are. A man who knows what he wants, who respects her, and who isn't afraid to express himself. That's how you get the woman you're looking for. Don't be too cool to gas up the woman you're dating. If you don't appreciate her, there's always some other man waiting in the wings who will. As you know, "One man's trash is another man's treasure."

KEY 14: DON'T CHASE, REPLACE (WALK AWAY)

You've got to know when to throw in the towel and recognize when she's just not that into you. This might sound a little harsh, but it's real talk. I don't want you out here wasting your valuable time on someone who isn't giving you the time of day. Okay, now I'm going to be tough on you. The chase isn't complicated. All you've got to do is want the woman who wants you back. A lot of men don't want to hear this, but you've got to get this in your head and get it clear. Especially if you're going all out taking her on dates, buying her gifts, checking in, and putting in the effort only for her to treat you like an afterthought. You've got to know when to cut your losses.

In the business world, there's a saying: "Don't throw good money after bad." Investors and entrepreneurs know this well. When a project or investment isn't working out, the smartest move is often to cut your losses and redirect your time, energy, and resources to something with better potential. It sounds simple, but that decision requires discipline. You may have already put a lot of money and effort into the venture, but the longer you hold on, the more it drains from you without giving back. Instead of clinging to a failing prospect, it's wiser to refocus on something that might actually pay off.

Dating is no different. Think of your time and energy like currency. Just as you wouldn't keep pouring money into a losing stock, you shouldn't keep investing in someone who isn't reciprocating. You've already given her your attention, perhaps taken her out, and maybe even gone the extra mile to show her you're interested. But if she isn't giving that energy back, then ask yourself, "What am I losing trying to get with this woman?"

Be real with yourself. How many times have you spent your energy on someone even when you knew deep down it wasn't going anywhere? Men waste time, energy, and money on women who aren't reciprocating their interest, who aren't on the same page, and who honestly just aren't worth the hassle. There's a saying, "Where there's a fair exchange, there's no robbery." If you're giving and giving, and she's barely throwing anything back your way, she's robbing you of your time and effort. And the longer you stay hooked, the harder it gets to see the reality right in front of you.

Sometimes, it's as simple as you and her just don't hit it off. Maybe it's clear after a few dates, or even the first one. You might find you've got nothing in common, or maybe you're headed in totally different directions in life. She might want a serious relationship, and you don't. Maybe she might want kids, and you're not about it. If this is hitting close to home, consider this chapter a therapy session, and if you're looking for a sign to turn your attention elsewhere, well, here it is.

You can't fit a square peg into a round hole. Stop forcing things that don't work. If she's not vibing with your authentic self, if she's lukewarm about who you are and what you bring, don't chase, replace. Remember the 2009 Rom-Com movie "*He's Just Not That Into You*"? Well, for this book, let's flip the title: "*She's Just Not That Into You.*" And that's okay. I need you to hear this because the last thing I want is for you to waste time, look silly, or worse, get played for a fool. Too many guys chase when they should have been replaced, and it costs them their confidence and respect. You've got to keep your dignity in the dating game and as a man. Knowing when to walk is part of that.

Now, let's get real about the "chasing" part. There's a difference between showing interest and looking desperate, and you need to be smart enough to tell when she's genuinely interested versus when she's giving you the runaround. Tupac said it best, "I don't want it if it's that easy." Don't get me wrong, there's nothing wrong with pursuing a woman, making your interest known, and going after what you want. But if she's not giving back that same energy after you've shown her you're serious, then it's time to do one of those 180 drifts like in the *Fast and Furious* movies and head in a different direction.

So, now you ask me, "Well, how do I know a woman wants me?" It's easy. If a woman's interested, she'll let you know. She'll respond, engage, and match whatever energy you give her. Simply put, she'll meet you halfway. If she's not doing any of that, she's either not into you or she's getting some kind of ego boost from stringing you along. Be real with yourself and watch for signs. If she never calls, rarely texts first, leaves you on read, dodges plans, or always has an excuse when you suggest hanging out, then she does not give a damn about you. That's not "playing hard to get" that's called wasting your time. She's finessing you, and draining your resources.

Remember how I told you about the women who go out with men just for a free meal? There are crazier stories out there, even on social media, of women trying to get men to take them to expensive, high-end restaurants and have the audacity to get mad if he doesn't. I don't want anyone ungrateful, and neither should you. Who doesn't appreciate The Cheesecake Factory? (A viral story of a woman mad at her date for choosing The Cheesecake Factory) Their menu is huge! That's diabolical, but that's reality. A lot of women are doing this every single day.

Look, life's busy for all of us. We've all got work, family, hobbies, and responsibilities, but if someone wants you in their life, they'll make time. That's the bottom line. You've got to match her energy. Once you've put in effort to get to know her, break the ice, and make plans, take note of her response. If she's never making an effort to reach out, then you fall back. It's a simple rule: if the energy isn't there, meet her where she's at and keep moving forward. It should be give and take. The Yin and the Yang. You should be getting as much as you're giving.

I've had plenty of moments where I thought I made a great connection with a woman, only to notice she never calls or initiates conversation even after I texted her multiple times to get to know her. You know what I did? I deleted her number. No second messages, no waiting around for a reply. If she's not showing the same level of interest, I'm not sticking around, no matter how attractive she is. Time is too valuable to waste on someone who's not as invested in me as I am in them. There are plenty of other women who will appreciate your attention and value the time you're offering. God didn't make just one. You've got options. Let her know that, and let her see that if she's not interested, there's someone else who will be.

I live by the simple principle, "You can't miss what you never had," so don't make the mistake of wanting someone so much that you're willing to be taken for granted. Keep your standards high. A strong man respects himself enough to walk away from anything that wastes his time. You've got to know when to let go and when to let the cream rise to the top. Meet them where they meet you, and don't ever be afraid to fall back if she's not giving you the same energy.

There's a scene in the movie "*Heat*" that hits home for me. Al Pacino, who plays a detective, is finally on the trail of Robert De Niro, a big-time bank robber. The only dilemma for De Niro's character is that he has one last job to take care of before he gets away, so he leaves his girlfriend in the car to wait in an alley while he goes to take care of this one last job. When he comes back to the car, he sees Pacino nearby. He has to make a choice and decides to walk away, leaving her behind so he won't get caught. It's just a movie, but it's got a lesson buried in there. Sometimes, no matter how invested you are physically or emotionally, or how much you've put in, you have to walk away when the situation demands it. You can't keep ignoring the signs.

Find women who share the same level of interest in you that you have in them. There's also a psychological component to this. Part of this is about confidence and having the mindset that she's not the only option. Sometimes you can't always show your hand. You have to have a poker face when you like or you're attracted to someone. Keep them guessing. They also have to know they can be replaced, and that you'll walk away at any moment. Even though you may be head over heels for them. Don't be so quick to wear your emotions on your sleeve. When she knows you're capable of walking away, she'll value the time she spends with you that much more. You're not out here to beg for attention.

Especially in the dating phase, don't be so quick to put your emotions out there. If you rush to show your interest and feelings too hard and too fast, you're setting yourself up to lose your leverage. You're allowed to be intrigued without putting everything on the line. Don't be the man who proposes marriage on the first date. And yes, that actually happened to someone I know. It was embarrassing for her, but even more so embarrassing for him because, of course, she said no and never went on a date with him again.

Keep your cool and stay in control. If she's genuinely interested, she'll put in effort too, and you'll see the difference. So don't be afraid to let her pursue you a bit. Let her be the one to ask what you're up to, to see if you're available. There's always going to be someone out there who sees what you bring to the table and respects you for it. Don't chase someone who doesn't.

KEY 15: DON'T BE WEIRD (RED FLAGS)

When it comes to dating, nothing is a quicker deal-breaker than a guy who comes off as weird, creepy, or just plain awkward. It's one of the biggest reasons you might find yourself blocked or ghosted, and it's exactly why this chapter is necessary. We live in a world where access to women is easier than ever, thanks to dating apps, social media, and messaging apps. But with that access comes a certain responsibility. Women have to be cautious with their time and attention, especially these days when dating apps, social media, and technology mean that practically anyone can try to connect with them. That's why it's crucial to avoid behaviors that might make you seem like a "red flag" in her eyes, especially when you're just starting to get to know each other.

Now, you might be thinking, "I'm not creepy." And maybe you aren't. But sometimes, it's not always clear what can seem weird or off-putting to someone you've just met. In this chapter, I'll walk you through some specific behaviors that turn women off or make them feel uncomfortable. I want you to avoid coming off as a red flag by showing you what they are in the first place. These are based on real-life stories from women who've experienced these things firsthand. So let's keep you out of the "weird zone," my friend because it's easy to get in it, but almost impossible to get out.

First off, you have to have some tact in how you approach a woman. When you're trying to get a woman's attention in public, there's a right and a wrong way to do it. I'll be the first to admit, I've been guilty of making catcalls in the past. But Catcalling is not the move. Most men know what I mean by "cat calls," but just in case you don't, it's that whistle or random shout-out that is honestly not as charming as you might think it is. If you want to approach a woman respectfully, keep it simple. Try saying, "Excuse me, miss" or "Hi, I just wanted to introduce myself." If she's interested, she'll respond. If not, let her be.

If you manage to catch her attention, don't mess it up with inappropriate or obscene comments. There's a huge difference between a respectful compliment and an off-the-wall remark. "You look amazing" is fine. "Now, that's a fat a**" is not. You barely know that woman. What made you think talking about her butt right off the bat is a great look? This sounds like obvious advice, but women have truckloads of stories about men saying inappropriate things to them.

I've talked about the importance of giving a woman compliments in prior chapters. At any point, did I tell you to compliment a stranger on her butt or anything of the sort? No. Because no woman wants to be sexualized by a stranger. If she's just going about her day and some random guy walks up to her or calls out to her from across the street, making obscene remarks about her body, she immediately thinks she's in danger. Such behavior makes you come off as aggressive when you should be a smooth operator.

Okay, this makes sense, right? But what if you shoot your shot online and slid into her DMs? Social media and dating apps are where many guys trip up. If you're messaging a woman, sending multiple DMs without a response is a red flag.

Nothing screams "desperate" louder than bombarding a woman with DMs, especially if she's not responding. Don't keep messaging, asking why she's not returning your messages. That's annoying. She doesn't owe you a response, so if she doesn't reply, take it as a sign that she's not interested and move on. Most guys don't take rejection well (which I discuss in length in the chapter on "Rejection"), but it's important to remember that "no" is a part of dating. You HAVE to learn how to be okay with being told "no." Don't become a cyberstalker or a cyber bully, or get into the habit of harassing a woman who rejects you. The more you try to push after rejection, the more uncomfortable it makes her, and it can lead to you getting blocked or even reported. Keep your dignity, and move on when it's clear she's not interested. You have to get some no's, to get a yes. Take that approach.

I have female friends who show me guys they've had to block for this type of behavior. Or, the men in their DM's that are talking to themselves because the woman hasn't responded. It's honestly sad and gives off those stalker vibes. Give her time to respond to your first message. If she doesn't respond, once again, take it as a sign that she's not interested and move on.

Another thing you should never do, and this is guaranteed to raise a red flag, is randomly calling a woman on social media that you've never even met. Believe it or not, some guys think it's okay to video call a woman out of the blue on social media apps. It sounds obvious, but a lot of guys do it, and every woman I know hates it. Randomly video-calling a stranger is intrusive and feels like a red flag right off the bat. Even FaceTiming too early can be off-putting if you haven't established a good connection yet. Why would someone you've never met answer your video call? It sounds crazy but some men actually do this. As you may have guessed, this tactic or approach is never received well by women and who can blame them? You must establish some sort of foundation and rapport first before using that method of making contact.

This should go without saying, but sending unsolicited pictures of your "Johnson" (that's your man tool) is one of the quickest ways to get blocked and labeled as a creep. Even if you think it's flattering, trust me, it's not. No matter how well-endowed you think you are. I don't know where this "move" came from or why some men still think it works. Most, if not all, women don't find this appealing at all. If anything, in this new age, women view this as harassment. For one, you've already crossed several boundaries in one move. Not only does it come off as disrespectful, but it also shows a lack of judgment and maturity. Trying this won't only get you blocked but you'll likely earn a bad reputation that will be hard to shake.

You'd think that's the worst move, but I can tell you there are men out here who show up to a woman's workplace or home unannounced. Even if things are going well, you should never just "pop by" without an invitation. Respect her space and her comfort levels, especially if you're still in the early stages of getting to know each other. The only exception to this rule is if you're already in a relationship and she has permitted you to do this. Consent, consent, consent. As I write this book, I can tell you the women I may go out with, none of them would show up at my place unannounced or without calling, even if it's someone I'm comfortable with. Showing up announced crosses a dangerous boundary that is hard to come back from.

I'd go as far as to say that even sending flowers or gifts can feel like too much too soon if you haven't developed a real connection yet. You don't want to come off too strong. Give things time to grow naturally. After some time, when she feels comfortable with you, she will appreciate gestures like sending her flowers, candy, or other gifts. But if you want to do something nice for her, check in first and make sure she's okay with it. If you move too quickly, you risk overwhelming her and sending her running in the opposite direction.

Speaking of moving too quickly, something I mentioned in the last chapter, "Don't Chase, Replace," about a guy proposing on the first date. This falls into the "red flag" and "weird" category. A friend finally goes on a date with a guy she has been talking to. Midway through the date, the guy gets on one knee and proposes in front of everyone!! Talk about jumping the gun! Needless to say, she said no, and never called him again after pulling such a stunt.

Unless you're on the latest episode of "Married At First Sight," you shouldn't be busting out the engagement ring on a first date.

Another thing that you may not think is a red flag or a little weird on a date, is talking about your ex. Exes are exes for a reason. This can make a woman uncomfortable if you're constantly talking about your ex-girlfriend. Men do it, I've been guilty of it. If she notices that you bring your ex up a lot, she's going to automatically assume that you're not over her. Unless your date asks about past dealings, it shouldn't be a topic of discussion. And God forbid you draw any comparison between your new potential love interest and your ex-girlfriend. You can probably forget about going out on another date with her. She's not there to compete with someone she doesn't even know.

If there's one thing you take away from this chapter, it's that sometimes, the best way to show you're a solid guy is by being cool and relaxed, especially at the beginning. Trying too hard, pushing too much for attention, or coming on too strong will backfire. When you can make a woman feel comfortable, she'll naturally let her guard down. But if you're coming across as intense or overbearing, that guard goes up quickly. If you've ever watched different Lifetime movies, you know that they're filled with stories of obsessive men who exhibit weird and creepy behavior towards women, and it never ends well.

Stay out of the "weird zone," read the room, and show her you're the kind of guy she should be with. The behaviors and actions described in this chapter will surely have you on the outside looking in if you're not careful. I have other examples like a guy pulling out his phone charger on a date at a restaurant to charge his phone. Please charge your phone before you leave home. If there are too many of these red flags you're almost assured to not get another date.

KNOCK IT OUT THE PARK (SEX) *BONUS KEY

Alright, let's get into the big topic that's probably been in the back of your mind this whole time... sex. I could write a whole book on sex, and I know there are already tons out there. But for this book, let's treat this as a bonus chapter. Let's get into it!

Sex eventually becomes a part of dating when there is a genuine connection and physical attraction. Also, if you're becoming a dating savant by applying the keys I discuss in this book. Whether you're out to increase your body count or aiming to find lasting love. This chapter isn't about every nuance, position, or technique. It's about setting the stage for when the moment comes, addressing sex from a dating perspective, and giving you a few essentials to get the job done right. Because let's face it, if you're putting in all the work to connect with women, you want to make sure you make it to the finish line.

Let's start by getting one thing straight because we've got to be on the same page here: sex is like the icing on the cake, but it's not the whole cake itself. Everything I've discussed in this book up to this point is the actual cake. Communication, chemistry, being a gentleman, respect, conversation, being honest, etc. all of that is what really matters when you're trying to connect with a woman. *That's the cake.* You build the foundation first. Then, when you've done the work and both of you are feeling that connection, sex becomes the extra layer that makes everything even better.

Of course, some relationships are all icing and have no substance, meaning the sex is what the whole relationship is based on. You've got to know the difference. There's nothing wrong with enjoying the physical side, but know what you're getting into. If it's only about the "icing," don't expect it to turn into a relationship.

Men are visual creatures, right? We've talked about this throughout this book. One of the issues with being visual creatures, however, is we sometimes get carried away by what we see and try to reverse-engineer a relationship. By this, I mean we make sex the foundation, then try to work our way back to the important things like conversation. If you've ever hooked up with a woman and then tried to turn that hookup into a long-term situation, you'll know what I'm talking about. The sex came way too fast, without you even really getting to know each other, and now it's a mess because you didn't have anything in common with this person in the first place. It was purely physical.

Sex is the adult playground of sensuality and exploration. It's the natural intimate human experience, that two individuals share who are attracted to each other physically, mentally, and emotionally. Sometimes the attraction can be purely physical, as stated above.

There have been times I had nothing in common with a woman, but there was an underlying physical attraction. It happens. However, when the connection is felt on all three levels, it makes for an amazing sexual experience.

The best sexual experiences come from paying attention to what your partner wants and needs. So, at some point during the dating phase, when things start heating up, it's smart to talk about what both of you like in the bedroom. Yeah, that means discussing preferences in the bedroom. It doesn't have to be awkward. It's better to be upfront and know what she's into— and what you're into— beforehand. Ask about her favorite positions, what turns her on, and so on. These are essential conversations that will pay off when things get intimate.

When that moment comes and presents itself, that she's finally ready to be intimate with you, you have to be ready to knock it out of the park. You've got to drop the proverbial hammer. Now, if you're sitting there wondering how you'll know when the "right time" is, I say pay attention to the signs. It won't be a mystery. When a woman is comfortable and trusts you, she'll send subtle cues. It might be the way she playfully touches you repeatedly or the way she leans into you or how the conversations shift to becoming more sexual. So, if you're noticing a lot of playful touching and lingering glances, get ready to make your move.

Look, no pressure, but you do *not* want to be the guy who underdelivers when the moment finally arrives. A woman will talk, and you don't want to be the guy getting roasted in the group chat because you didn't put it down. This puts a lot of pressure on you as a man, but remember, if you've built a strong connection, you're already more than halfway there.

But don't rush in. Women can decide early on if they're interested in being intimate with a guy, but they won't always act on it right away. Some of them can know from the first date, others by the second or third. They're waiting to see if you're the kind of guy who respects their pace, their comfort, and if you're worth letting in that way. Play it cool, show her respect, and let things flow naturally. Never try to force the issue.

Before we get to the business, make sure there is consent. I can't stress this enough. Flirting, touching, or even suggestive language is not consent. Maybe back in the day, this would be considered consent, but not anymore. Sure, if she's making the first move, unbuckling your pants, stripping down, and really going for it, this qualifies as consent. But I would go as far as to say, make sure you have some sort of verbal consent. Even if she's super eager to get down. Too many men have suffered the consequences of not getting verbal consent, so even if you forget everything else in this chapter, don't forget about this.

So, now she's finally ready to go there. You've worked up to this point, the chemistry is there, and the moment is heated. Now what? If you're reading this book, I'm going to assume you're not a virgin, but if you happen to be one or maybe have very little sexual experience, I'm going to give you a few tips. These tips are for seasoned veterans as well.

First, make sure you have protection. How many stories have you heard, where guys didn't have sex with a woman because he forgot a condom? I think this has happened to every man at some point. I know I'm guilty. My second piece of advice is to take your time. This isn't a sprint, and she doesn't want you coming on too fast. Take your time with every part of the process, starting with setting the right mood. Music can be a game-changer here— romantic, smooth tunes can take things from zero to sixty pretty quickly. Light a candle, set the vibe, and make her feel special. Women want to be caressed, nurtured, and seduced, so it's your job to create an atmosphere that makes them feel wanted and attractive.

From there, you can start with kissing. I love slow sensual kissing. It's like starting the car and warming it up. There's nothing like a good, slow, sensual kiss to get things started, then gradually work your way down to other sensitive spots, like her neck or ears. Pay attention to how she reacts, and spend a bit more time on the spot she's most responsive. Don't rush it. Make the experience about her, and let her responses guide you. Let your hands do some work too, rubbing her thighs, lower back, breasts, and or the back of her neck. Look her in the eyes, show her you're fully present. Engage her like you're fully into it— because you should be.

For the sake of keeping this chapter as PG as possible, let's just say you know what comes next. At this point, she should be worked up into a frenzy. Ready for you in any and every way possible. All that talk you had before about her preferences? This is where it pays off. Listen to her body language, her sounds, her breathing, and any little cues she gives you. Every woman's different, so don't assume what worked on another woman will work with her. Treat each experience like it's new, and tune into what she's feeling. Think of it like following GPS directions. You wouldn't ignore the directions to get to your desired destination, would you? Of course not. If you want to reach your destination and help her climax, listen to the guidance she's given you.

Now you know about the starting and the ending, so let's talk about all the bits in between for a second— sixty seconds, to be precise. Some of you already know where I'm going with this. One of the quickest ways to fail in the bedroom is performance. You do *not* want to be the one-minute man. While there is some debate, depending on who you talk to, on how long good sex should last, it's certainly not one minute. A woman wants to be satisfied in the bedroom, and that's your job. You've got to perform long enough to satisfy her. Like I said, this isn't a sprint. If you want to make a real impact, take it slow, focus on different areas, and switch things up. Practice deep breathing if you need to control yourself. Switching positions also helps you last longer. And pace yourself. Don't be afraid to slow things down and focus on other areas of her body if you need to take a break. You don't have to keep the same tempo. You're not a machine. A good rule of thumb is to alternate between two or three positions per session. Don't master five positions and try to perform them all at once. That's exhausting. Remember, this isn't a final exam— stay present, stay connected to her, and just enjoy yourself.

If you're worried about physical issues like getting it up or stamina, there's no shame in seeking help. Consider talking to a doctor if it's affecting your confidence or performance. There are also natural supplements that might support stamina and energy like ginseng, maca root, tongkat ali, and ashwagandha, just to name a few. You have to think of your body as a high-performance race car. What you put in affects what you get out, especially when it comes to sex. Keep yourself in shape, stay hydrated, and take care of your mental health. Do the things necessary to be at peak performance before it gets to that point of being intimate with whomever you are dating. Plus, the confidence you'll gain from taking care of yourself will naturally make you more attractive to women.

When it comes down to it, sex should be an extension of the connection you've built. The icing on the cake. Don't overthink it, don't put too much pressure on yourself. Be confident in the groundwork you've laid and the chemistry you've built, and trust that you've got this. So take this advice, apply it, and when that time comes you're going to put it down and give her a reason to keep coming back for more.

CONCLUSION

So, you made it! Congrats! I hope you've gained some real and valuable insights to help you navigate the often crazy world of dating. As you know, it can feel like a maze with a plethora of dating apps, matchmaking services, speed-dating events across various cities and so much more. I felt like giving men an edge in the dating landscape was necessary. That's why equipping yourself with the knowledge and tactics covered in this book is crucial.

My goal was to keep everything as relatable and straightforward as possible for every man— no matter your race, religion, background, political affiliation, economic status, or job type, whether blue-collar or white-collar. These principles are universal when it comes to the dating game. Possessing the necessary mindset and approach and not just knowing how to treat them right, but engaging with them in a real and refreshing way. I shared my personal stories and real-life examples to help you grow into the kind of man who naturally attracts the women you want and helps you become the Casanova you want to be.

As you've read already, it all starts with becoming the best version of yourself. Don't ever forget that. That's why the first chapter of this book is dedicated to making you a better man. As men, we should all strive to get 1% better every day. It's simply the law of attraction. You attract what you become. So, if you want a certain caliber of woman, become the kind of man who belongs in her world. Eagles soar with eagles. You never see them hanging around with pigeons, do you? To find the right partner, you need to soar high and become someone worth connecting with on that level. In other words, if you want to elevate, you must do the necessary work to get there. Your mindset is everything, not just in dating but in life.

Throughout this book, I've woven personal development into every chapter because it's often the missing ingredient in dating success. It's easy to overlook, but when you feel good about yourself, your confidence levels grow, and this is attractive to women. I talked a lot about building yourself up— mentally, financially, and emotionally. Even if you remove dating from the equation, becoming "whole" in these areas gives you a solid foundation to build on, no matter what your goals may be. Some guys miss these basics, blindly going from one dating disaster to the next, wondering why they're always struggling, making mistakes that could've been avoided if they'd put in the work on themselves first.

As I said in the introduction, this book is meant to be your ultimate wingman. Like a good wingman, he's always got your back. Anytime you need a refresher, flip back to these pages. If you're struggling with rejection, go over that chapter again. If you're not feeling confident? Read the chapter on confidence until the words become a part of you. Don't just read this book once and let it gather dust. Go through it a second, even third time. Each time you revisit these chapters, you'll probably pick up on something you missed before. No matter where you are on your dating journey, this book is here to help you move from A to Z. We even covered the importance of planning and the little details that make a big impression.

I want you to learn to have more fun with dating. Laugh a little if you've struggled with that. In the chapter, "Why So Serious," I talked about how dating doesn't have to feel like a job interview, so just relax, take a deep breath, and have fun with it. The more women you talk to and dates you go on, the better and more comfortable you'll become at dating. It's a skill that takes practice, trial, and error. Maybe after reading this book, you'll see some of the ways you tripped up in the past. If you see where you've gone wrong on past dates, there might be an opportunity for you to reconnect with someone you liked and maybe messed things up with. Sometimes, a genuine apology for your missteps can open the door to a second chance with her.

When you apply the principles in each chapter, you'll find yourself more prepared, more desirable, and better equipped to set yourself apart from other guys in her eyes. You won't just be another guy she dates. You want to be the man who makes a lasting impression. You'll become a high-value man, and I can tell you from experience that women want a high-value man because he's a confident man who knows how to treat a woman right. Let me let you in on a little secret— a high-value man doesn't chase, he chooses.

If this book has been a valuable read to you, pass it on. Share it with friends, colleagues, family members, or anyone you think could benefit. Plenty of single men might secretly struggle with the topics covered here. Whether they're young guys in college or older men re-entering the dating world, every man should have a solid foundation in knowing how to interact with and treat a woman. I know there's a lot of advice out there about dating— books, podcasts, social media pages, etc. So it's easy to get overwhelmed. I hope this book has been and continues to be, a practical and grounded source for you.

Now that you've got all this knowledge— scratch that— now that you've got all these 15 keys, plus one bonus key, it's time to get to work and put them into action. There's no time like the present. So if you've been sitting around, stagnant and not motivated, let this book put the battery in your back to get going and get active. The woman of your dreams is not going to come to you. Put yourself out there for the universal law of attraction to get to work now that you'll be equipped. Remember, you can be the guy who gets the girl, but you have to have the necessary tools in your toolbox, to get the job done right. Dating For Men Made Easy gives you those tools.

www.ingramcontent.com/pod-product-compliance
Lightning Source LLC
Chambersburg PA
CBHW070536030426
42337CB00016B/2222